Local
Story

LOCAL STORY

*The Massie-Kahahawai Case
and the Culture of History*

JOHN P. ROSA

UNIVERSITY OF
HAWAI'I PRESS
HONOLULU

LIBRARY OF CONGRESS CATALOGING-IN-PUBLICATION DATA

Rosa, John P., author.

Local story : the Massie-Kahahawai case and the culture of history /
John P. Rosa.

p. cm.

Includes bibliographical references and index.

ISBN 978-0-8248-2825-7 (cloth : alk. paper)

ISBN 978-0-8248-3970-3 (pbk. : alk. paper)

1. Fortescue, Grace, 1883–1979—Trials, litigation, etc. 2. Massie, Thomas H.—
Trials, litigation, etc. 3. Massie, Thalia, 1911–1963. 4. Trials (Murder)—Hawaii—
History—20th century. 5. Trials (Rape)—Hawaii—History—20th century. 6.
Kahahawai, Joseph, 1909–1932. 7. Lynching—Hawaii—History—20th century. 8.
Hawaii—Race relations—History—20th century. 9. Hawaii—History—1900–1959.
I. Title.

KF224.F685R67 2014

364.152'3092—dc23

2013042621

Designed by Julie Matsuo-Chun
Printed by Thomson-Shore, Inc.

*For
generations
of family*

CONTENTS

IX   Acknowledgements

1   **INTRODUCTION:** The Massie-Kahahawai Case as a Local Story

9   **CHAPTER 1:** Local Boys: Ahakuelo, Chang, Ida, Kahahawai, and Takai as the Accused

26   **CHAPTER 2:** Haole Woman: Thalia Massie and the Defense of White Womanhood

44   **CHAPTER 3:** The Killing of Joseph Kahahawai: Native Hawaiians and Stories of Resistance

65   **CHAPTER 4:** A Closing and an Opening: The Massie-Fortescue Murder Trial

77   **CHAPTER 5:** Story, Memory, History

102   **EPILOGUE:** *Haʻina ʻia mai*

109   Chronology of the Massie-Kahahawai Case and Its Legacy
117   Notes
137   Bibliography
153   Index

ACKNOWLEDGMENTS

Many people helped with the researching and writing of this book—and many more provided collegial, moral, and familial support over the years as I developed as an educator and scholar in Hawai'i and the continental United States. Some of the teachers who encouraged me to write about issues of race, ethnicity, and identity are Yong Chen, Dorothy Fujita-Rony, John Liu, and Jon Wiener of the University of California, Irvine. Colleagues in the field of Asian American and ethnic studies such as George Lipsitz, Tom Nakayama, Franklin Odo, and George Okihiro have been particularly supportive in helping me navigate the waters of academia. Scholars of Pacific Islanders in the United States such as Amy Stillman, Vince Diaz, and Damon Salesa provided a chance to discuss the histories of Hawai'i, Oceania, and the sea of islands during meetings at Ann Arbor, Michigan. Workshop settings coordinated by Geoff White at the East-West Center and Yujin Yaguchi from the Center for Pacific and American Studies at the University of Tokyo were also special venues to share research as it developed.

Friends from Kamehameha Schools–Kapālama welcomed me and my family back to Honolulu in 2006 when I jumped into teaching secondary school students and re-learned what it means to work with youngsters in twenty-first-century Hawai'i. Mahalo nui loa to Julian Ako, Amy Kimura,

Kapua Akiu-Wilcox, Jan Becket, Richard Hamasaki, Kawika Makanani, and especially ʻUmi Perkins.

Faculty, staff, and students from so many departments at the University of Hawaiʻi at Mānoa were instrumental in helping me re-think what it means to live and work in Hawaiʻi as an engaged scholar. In my home Department of History, Karen Jolly, Matthew Lauzon, and Matthew Romaniello were just a few of the many faculty who welcomed me on board in 2008. As a specialist in the history of modern Hawaiʻi, I am honored to join Noelani Arista, David Chappell, and David Hanlon in adding to our department's Hawaiʻi/Pacific focus.

The Department of Ethnic Studies helped to shape and nurture me, showing me by example how to work with and listen to Hawaiʻi's multiple communities. Thank you to Brahim Aoude, the late Marion Kelly, Noel Kent, Rod Labrador, Ty Tengan, and Lisa Uperesa. Davianna Pōmaikaʻi McGregor and Jonathan Okamura were especially helpful in reading and commenting on chapter drafts. As long-standing members of the Association for Asian American Studies, they also encouraged me to present my work at conferences for more than a decade. Other AAAS members such as Theodore Gonsalves (formerly of American Studies) and Karen Umemoto (Urban Planning) provided a generous push whenever I needed to get going again.

In the English Department, Craig Howes, Paul Lyons, Rodney Morales, and Gary Pak stirred me to think about how issues of place, story, and history all overlap in the *moʻolelo* that are told here in the islands. Jonathan Kay Kamakawiwoʻole Osorio of Hawaiian Studies has been a role model in showing how academic history can also be of service to a larger public. In the College of Education, Eileen Tamura and Jeff Moniz shared their expertise on curriculum development in Hawaiʻi. Lois Yamauchi, also from Education, showed me around her home on Kahawai Street that the Massies lived in during the 1930s.

At the Hawaiian and Pacific Collection of UH Mānoa's Hamilton Library, Joan Hori, Jodie Mattos, Dore Minatodani, and Chieko Tachihata helped me track down information, as did the expert staff at the Hawaiʻi State Archives and the San Bruno branch of the National Archives and Records Administration. I owe a great thanks to those who have also researched the case, such as Cobey Black, Dennis Carroll, the late Glen Grant, David Stannard, and Mark Zwonitzer. Mahalo nui loa to Masako Ikeda, Ann Ludeman, Susan Corrado, and Kathleen Paparchontis, who moved the manuscript through the process at UH Press.

This book is dedicated to generations of family—for the stories related to us by our families are often the first ones to teach us what "history" is all about. Mahalo nui loa to Uncle Kekuni Blaisdell, a friend and mentor whose own father was a juror in one of the trials of the case. Thank you also to friends and relatives of those mentioned in the case: Aonani Ahakuelo-Chernisky, Deena Ahakuelo, Kim Kahahawai Farrant, Tara Kahahawai, Luwella Leonardi, the late Ah Quon McElrath, Nanette Napoleon, and Miriam Woolsey Reed, who are just a few who shared their deeply personal family stories.

I owe a great thanks to my extended ʻohana: my grandparents, Gertrude and Leon Chock, my parents, Cynthia and Richard Johnson, and the Rosa, Yim, and Okimoto clans. My immediate family members Jolyn, Mei, and Luke should also know that I could not have finished this project without them. Thank you—I love you dearly.

The Massie-Kahahawai Case
as a Local Story

IN THE FALL of 1931 and the early months of 1932, the events of the Massie case shook the Territory of Hawai'i to its very core. In September 1931 five local working-class youths in Hawai'i found themselves in the midst of a shocking predicament. Joseph "Kalani" Kahahawai, Benedict "Benny" Ahakuelo, Horace Ida, David Takai, and Henry Chang stood accused of raping a white woman in Waikīkī. Their case took place fewer than six months after the first trial of the Scottsboro Boys in Alabama. There, nine African American boys were accused of raping two white women on a westbound train traveling from Scottsboro to Memphis, Tennessee. In both the Scottsboro and Massie cases, whites expressed their anxiety and anger when they believed that nonwhite men had broken the "unwritten law" separating them from white women.

In the Massie case, Thalia Massie, the twenty-year-old wife of a naval lieutenant stationed at Pearl Harbor, alleged that she had been dragged into a car on the night of September 12, taken to a remote location, and raped by "some Hawaiian boys." Though she initially told police that she could not identify her assailants' faces, within twelve hours of the attack she asserted that the five young men whom the police had marched before her hospital bed were the ones who had assaulted her. A mishandling of evidence, shoddy police work, and contradictory testimony led to a mistrial when the case was

1

brought to court in November 1931. But before a second trial could be convened, there were two acts of vigilantism. In December a group of U.S. Navy men kidnapped one of the accused, Horace Ida, beat him, and threatened to throw him over the Pali lookout if he did not confess to the rape of Thalia Massie. Ida refused and miraculously managed to escape with his life. In early January 1932, however, Joseph Kahahawai was not so fortunate. Thalia Massie's husband, Thomas, her mother, Grace Fortescue, and two navy men (Edward Lord and Albert Jones) kidnapped Kahahawai and killed him with a single gunshot to the chest, piercing his heart.

After the killing renowned lawyer Clarence Darrow agreed to defend the Massie-Fortescue group in what would be one of his last courtroom appearances. John C. Kelley, a young public prosecutor for the Territory, went head to head against Darrow and successfully convinced the jury to find the Massie-Fortescue group guilty of manslaughter. The fact that one of them had fired the shot that killed Kahahawai was undisputed. Several witnesses had seen a poorly disguised Thomas Massie, Grace Fortescue, and the two other men force Kahahawai into an automobile in downtown Honolulu on January 8, 1932. Later, when police pulled over Massie's Buick after a long car chase from downtown Honolulu to the easternmost coast of Oʻahu, their search of a laundry basket in the backseat revealed the naked body of Joseph Kahahawai.

The trial of *Territory of Hawaii v. Massie, Fortescue, Lord, and Jones* included the rather new defense tactic of using expert witnesses (or "alienists," as they were called) to assert that Thomas Massie had exhibited all the signs of "temporary insanity" when he fired the shot that killed Kahahawai. Darrow and his assistants were unable to convince the jury to acquit, but they were successful in urging the jury to reduce the Territory's charges of kidnapping and murder to the single, lesser charge of manslaughter. Though the racially mixed jury of local men also recommended leniency, Judge Charles Davis sentenced Thomas Massie, Grace Fortescue, Edward Lord, and Albert Jones to ten years of hard labor. Under considerable pressure from Congress and the U.S. Navy, however, Governor Lawrence McCully Judd promptly commuted their sentences. The convicted Massie-Fortescue group ended up serving only one hour—spent in the governor's office signing papers and sipping tea or drinking champagne, some say—before they were freed. Within a week all four had left the islands and never returned.

During 1931–1932 a set of criminal trials involving the alleged rape of a white woman and the killing of a Native Hawaiian man brought unexpected attention to Hawai'i and the people who lived there. This book tells a story about those events—the Massie-Kahahawai case, or the Massie case, as it has come to be known. Readers already familiar with it are not likely to learn many new "true crime" details since this book is not solely an account of the case. Instead, it examines how and why the case has often been portrayed in Hawai'i as a "local" story since the early 1930s. The book explores how the content of the case lent itself well to telling particular kinds of stories; it also examines the complexities of telling and retelling the case's historical events as a local incident in the islands as opposed to an American one that cast Hawai'i as merely a small outpost of the United States. In Hawai'i people of my generation and my parents' generation were largely unaware of the Massie-Kahahwai case until broader interest in it was revitalized around the mid-1980s. It was this prevailing silence that interested me in the first place. How could we and many others of our respective generations *not* have heard about it? After all, these events of the early 1930s involving an alleged rape and murder were sensationalized by newspapers in the islands and on the continental United States.

One might say that there is politics to history, since those in power always seem able to tell their version of the past. In contemporary Hawai'i, however, where people of different backgrounds often seek to avoid the appearance of conflict, "politics" might not be quite the right word. Instead, I have chosen to focus on the nature of historical storytelling—what I call "the culture of history." The word "culture" also suggests things that grow, that can be cultivated, and that people seek to sustain. History, after all, is not a dead or stagnant entity. Rather, it is alive—a set of active cultures and processes. In the islands people often speak of history as being close to their hearts; Native Hawaiians say that history can be felt in your *na'au*, your guts. When historians and other scholars trained in Western, empirical traditions rely only on written sources and printed documents, they frequently miss the powerful emotive elements of history found in oral and performative accounts. In seeking to bring a more organic approach to Hawai'i's history, I have spent a great deal of time talking story with people, taking part in community events, and exploring the relationships that people have to their pasts—and more importantly, to each other.

THE MASSIE-KAHAHAWAI CASE
AS A LOCAL STORY

I have organized the book in such a way to relate what I call a "local story" that pays attention to issues of place. It also examines how the immediate and the personal for local stories are tied to individual and group identities, linked intimately to families, neighborhoods, and ethnic communities. I use the term "story" instead of "history" in order to draw attention to the range of ways that progressions of events can be told. The case has been recounted in print culture (newspapers, history books, and novelizations), in dramatic forms (plays and historical reenactments), and as television productions (a miniseries and a PBS documentary). Using the term "story" also suggests the contestability of any account. Conversely, the word "history" often suggests a finality and fixedness to an account. In writing about story I hope to draw greater attention to how all accounts are often called into question and how historical storytelling is a process continually in the making.

Story does not necessarily mean a work of fiction. In piecing together a reliable narrative of the Massie-Kahahawai case, I used corroborating source materials found in places like the Hawai'i State Archives, in the National Archives and Records Administration (San Bruno branch), and in the Hawaiian-Pacific collection of the University of Hawai'i at Mānoa's Hamilton Library. We must remind ourselves that written and printed sources also should be subject to scrutiny, for these records of the past hold inconsistencies as well. When there are highly conflicting accounts of key events in the Massie case, I have presented the most plausible ones, clarifying when some individuals have probably leaned a little more to the side of speculation and rumor.

Telling a local story foregrounds Hawai'i perspectives—often those of Native Hawaiian, Asian, and other residents—privileging them over other versions of the Massie case that have focused on the American "national" perspectives of continental Americans like Thalia Massie and navy personnel stationed in the islands. Since the 1970s the story of the Massie-Kahahawai case has been told frequently as a kind of "local origins" story. The defendants in the case were of Native Hawaiian, Japanese, and Chinese Hawaiian ancestry and were lumped together as young men of color—especially when compared to Thalia Massie, a recently arrived haole (white) woman from the continental United States.

The Massie case and the stories it generated have been used to explain the formation of local identity in Hawai'i for many years. The case came at a crucial moment in the early 1930s, when Native Hawaiians, Asian immigrants, other working-class people of color, and their descendants found that they had common ground. At various points throughout this book readers might also see that it "talks story," in a way. The narrative of this book is not an oral one, of course, but it includes transcribed oral accounts and features them in relating parts of the Massie case and the larger history of Hawai'i. The practice of talking story is intimately tied to local identity: locals want to be able to tell you important stories—important histories—at their own pace and in their own fashion.

Throughout this book I speak very analytically and critically about the strengths and weaknesses of telling a local story. I explain that multiple stories and histories are told—ones that compete with each other—and that, increasingly in Hawai'i, it is the local ones that seem most relevant to Hawai'i audiences, rather than ones generated in keeping with viewpoints found on the continental United States.

THE ORIGINS OF LOCAL IDENTITY

I am not the first person to point to the Massie-Kahahawai case as the originator of the term "local" in Hawai'i. That distinction belongs to University of Hawai'i (UH) sociologist Andrew Lind and Eric Yamamoto (then an undergraduate), who, in the early 1970s, discussed matters of individual and group identity in Hawai'i when Yamamoto was completing his senior thesis, "From Japanee to Local," as part of the honors program at the university. As part of my own graduate training in the 1990s I looked at the genealogy of this local origins story and argued that the Massie-Kahahawai case was the first time the term "local" was used with any salience. I also outlined the parameters of local identity, building upon a framework advanced consistently by ethnic studies scholar Jonathan Okamura since the 1980s that highlighted a wide gap between whites and nonwhites that had emerged in the islands' plantation society. In 2000 I published my theory about the cultural production of local identity in *Amerasia,* a journal of Asian American studies in which Okamura and other scholars have written about Hawai'i's local society and culture since the early 1970s. In the article I clarified that in addition to racial and ethnic tensions, there were strong class distinctions that assisted in the formation of local identity. Particularly in the Massie case, there were divisions that overlapped into the analytical categories of gender and place as well.

During the first several years of the twenty-first century there was a resurgence of interest in the Massie-Kahahawai case for several reasons. Cobey Black, a longtime journalist who had been working on a book about the case since the early 1960s, published *Hawaii's Scandal* in 2002 with local publisher Island Heritage. In New York, filmmaker Mark Zwonitzer also embarked on crafting a television documentary about the case for WGBH Boston's series, the American Experience. In 2003 he consulted Black, UH American studies professor David Stannard, and me while preparing his hour-long documentary. Playwright and UH Theatre and Dance Department chair Dennis Carroll also produced his *Massie/Kahahawai* play for Kumu Kahua Theatre in early 2004, showing to sold-out audiences in Honolulu. Finally, in April 2005 Stannard's book, *Honor Killing,* was published on the same day that Zwonitzer's *The Massie Affair* premiered at the Hawaii International Film Festival.

As a result of the 2004–2005 appearances of a play, book, and documentary about the Massie-Kahahawai case, there has been a series of public discussions about it, along with the development of curricula for K-12 and university-level audiences that will be discussed later in this book. In chronicling this public history of the case, I also felt the need to assess the effects that writers like Stannard, Black, Carroll, and I have probably played as both participants and observers in the recent productions of memories regarding the case.

As a historian in the twenty-first century with access to numerous sources after the fact, I work with the benefit of hindsight. In retelling the case to you, the reader, I have thus assumed the role of a fairly omniscient storyteller who aims to relate the story to audiences, large and small, both in Hawai'i and on the continental United States. As the primary storyteller here, I am also a character in the story—for I have chosen what details to relate to you, determined which documents and other materials are more significant than others, and, in the past dozen years or so, found that I have also helped shape how others have interpreted and retold the case. In some ways this book takes off where Stannard left off. In his final chapter, "Prelude to Revolution," Stannard says that the case set the stage for a "revolution" in which locals would come to power as the *kama'āina* elite gradually gave way in the years leading up to statehood in 1959. I write of a revolution as well—specifically, one in the culture of history in Hawai'i where more voices can be heard in more places.

* * *

Each chapter presents a dialogue between the past and the present; each chapter is a kind of fractal in that it tells part of the story that can suggest the importance of the whole narrative. Chapters 1 and 2 illustrate the boundaries between Hawai'i's local population and white elites that helped fashion local identity. These chapters focus on differences between locals and nonlocals in social activities, values, and outlook, and introduce a spatialized argument by contrasting the Honolulu neighborhoods of Kalihi and Mānoa. Chapter 1 presents the young men accused of rape as a collective group known as the Kauluwela Boys, describes the activities of their youth in September 1931, and suggests how they came to be seen as Thalia Massie's assailants. Chapter 2 focuses on how Mrs. Massie left the safety of Mānoa Valley and became the case's first victim—not only because she was attacked on the night of September 12, but also because her own voice was often drowned out by various groups that aimed to defend "American womanhood" in the islands and assert "Southern honor."

Chapter 3 examines how locals and Native Hawaiians in particular viewed the killing of Joseph Kahahawai as an assault against peoples of color in Hawai'i in general at the hands of haoles, or whites. On the other hand, continental audiences had fewer personal connections to people in the case and were less likely to remember the Massie case after 1932. Chapter 4 shows how audiences on the continent forgot the case rather quickly; it was a tantalizing news story that faded from memory once another sensational news story, the kidnapping and murder of Charles Lindbergh's son in the spring of 1932, took its place. Chapter 4 also finishes the retelling of the case by recounting the last days of the Massie-Fortescue murder trial, the sentencing of the group, and the subsequent commutation of their sentences by Governor Lawrence McCully Judd in the spring of 1932. The chapter suggests how the end of the murder trial allowed continental American audiences to achieve a sense of closure, while also leaving an open wound to be remembered by local audiences in the islands for decades to come.

The aftermath of the Massie case has a history of its own and is addressed in the last third of the book in chapters examining how the case has survived in popular memory. Chapter 5 surveys popular renderings of the Massie case that have appeared in print, film, educational curricula, or live performances from the 1930s to the twenty-first century. This chapter shows that, more often than not, the public history versions of the case have contributed more to locals' understandings of what went on during 1931–1932; collective memories about the case have often been combinations of fact and fiction, given the widespread influence of popular versions of the case like the television miniseries *Blood and Orchids*.

Finally, I present an epilogue that brings the politics of local identity up to date. Here I discuss how local identity often involves recollections of the past that evoke emotions that usually go unrecorded by academic accounts of Hawai'i's history. At the very end of this book is a chronology of events that readers can turn to if they need assistance in making sense of the twists and turns of the Massie-Kahawahai case. The bibliography should help those who are interested in more detail about the case or about discussion of local historiography, local identity, and contemporary storytelling practices. These materials are meant to serve as guides; they are not definitive, but I have made them as extensive as possible, chronicling citations of the case up until 2012, some eighty years after the original events of the Massie-Kahahawai case.

1

LOCAL BOYS

Ahakuelo, Chang, Ida,
Kahahawai, and Takai
as the Accused

D. W. WATSON: All the haoles [whites] on the mainland are blaming
the Hawaiians, Ben. And these people that killed Joe blame you
fellows. They got one Hawaiian and Ben—you are going to be
next. They're going to get you just as sure as you are alive right
now. Even if it takes 10 years, you'll never know when you are li-
able to get it. Joe got off easy—they just shot him. The next time,
Ben, they're going to torture you fellows. It's going to be hell.

BEN AHAKUELO: I might as well die. I'm not afraid. If I was guilty I'd
feel funny but I don't. I'm going home and if they want to shoot
me, alright.

—*Conversation between D. W. Watson and Ben Ahakuelo at the Honolulu
Police Station,* WEDNESDAY, JANUARY 20, 1932, 2:10–3:15 P.M.[1]

DESPITE INTIMIDATION BY Detective Watson and appeals from others "in the
name of the Hawaiian people," Ben Ahakuelo held to his story that he and the
other Kauluwela Boys had not assaulted Thalia Massie on the night of September 12, 1931.[2] Ahakuelo was adamant that he, Joseph Kahahawai, David Takai,
Horace Ida, and Henry Chang were innocent. All five young men had enjoyed

a night in Waikīkī but were on their way home ("Kalihi way," they said) at the time Thalia Massie was assaulted. Through their words and actions, young men like Ben Ahakuelo asserted a solid pride in who they were and what they did and did not do. This chapter explores local identity in Hawai'i of the 1930s through a close examination of the men's testimony regarding the night of September 12 and observations made by social scientists, social workers, police detectives, and Pinkerton investigators regarding the local youth population. In retelling this part of the Massie case, the aspects of local identity highlighted here are markedly male oriented and frequently underscore the tension between local and white males. This chapter focuses on local males and their group activities in order to examine how a sense of geographic place and space contributed to the formation of local identity in the 1930s.

Though they were of varying ethnic backgrounds, the Kauluwela Boys saw the area of Honolulu known as Kalihi-Pālama as their home. The press had begun to call the young men the Ala Moana Boys, thus linking them to the assault of Thalia Massie in the Ala Moana area. Ben Ahakuelo, Henry Chang, Joseph Kahahawai, Horace Ida, and David Takai had called themselves the Kauluwela Boys since their days at Kauluwela Elementary School near Vineyard Street; by 1931 the "boys" were in their early twenties. Their working-class neighborhood brought them together and stood in stark contrast to the valley of Mānoa some two to three miles away, which already harbored exclusive residences for island elites.

Detective Watson's interrogation of Ben Ahakuelo reveals the antagonism between young men like Ahakuelo and haoles—whites both in Hawai'i and on the continental United States who held a privileged position of power due to their skin color. This opposition was carried out on a spatial dimension as well. Though this nonwhite/white conflict was not limited to young men alone, we do see the most evidence of tension and violence between young male locals and white authority figures. By following the movements of the Kauluwela Boys, we are able to examine the geography of Honolulu in the 1930s and begin to see how spatial oppositions contributed to the formation of local identity.

Previous work on the Massie case is inattentive to the development of local culture and society in the islands and its spatial dimensions. The three books that were published in the 1960s and the works by Cobey Black, David Stannard, and Mark Zwonitzer in the early twenty-first century all stand unambiguously on the side of Hawai'i's local population and attempt to present the lives of the Kauluwela Boys as fairly as possible. Authors Van Slingerland, Wright, and Packer and Thomas all see the events of 1931–1932 as exacerbated by a sensationalistic national press and lament the injustices perpetrated on Hawai'i's peoples.[3] Nevertheless, much of what has been written about the Massie case narrates it as mainly a political tragedy for the peoples of Hawai'i or a personal tragedy for all parties involved. In so doing, these "true crime" narratives focus more on the details of the case and have done little to highlight the contours of local identity that crystallized as a result.

THE STRUCTURE AND LANGUAGE OF LOCAL IDENTITY

In the lean years of the 1920s and 1930s—two decades before the attack on Pearl Harbor ushered the United States into World War II—a distinct, local youth culture emerged in Hawai'i. At the turn of the twentieth century the sons and daughters of plantation workers of different ethnicities moved off the plantations to settle in urban centers like Honolulu and Hilo. By the late 1920s and early 1930s their children came of age and placed a significant burden on a labor market already stretched thin by the Great Depression.[4] Filipino migration and the influx of military personnel also produced an unbalanced sex ratio of nearly two men to every one woman aged fifteen to twenty-four. According to University of Hawai'i sociologist Romanzo Adams, 1930 census figures for Honolulu County indicated that there were 28,166 men aged fifteen to twenty-four and only 13,083 women for the same age group. Adams estimated that the excess of 15,083 men was made up of roughly "10,000 white soldiers, sailors, and other personnel" and "3,000 male Filipino laborers, very few of whom were married."[5]

The creation of this multiethnic local identity was made possible, in part, by the structural antagonisms of oppositional population groups. Among young local males, for example, the distinct youth culture that emerged in Honolulu stood in clear opposition to the increasing numbers of white servicemen from the continent. Adams provides the best evidence of this demographic shift: he saw an "an exceedingly large percentage of [the Honolulu] population in this 'youth' age group." More precisely, sociologists like Adams identified and charted the development of this male youth population, since it was this group whose actions could threaten the stability of Honolulu. Especially during the Depression years, economic conditions and lack of schooling and employment opportunities exacerbated the situation. In 1933, in an annual report that he wrote for the Honolulu Police Department, Adams expressed his concerns most pointedly: "For the past few years there have existed acute financial difficulties in many of the homes which coupled with unemployment for the boy himself along with the fact that many of them have been barred from additional schooling has only added to the number of potential criminals." Creating more recreational facilities was seen as one solution to the perceived rise in criminality among the local male population. One year after the conclusion of the Massie case the police department established a prevention division to ward off crime.[6]

In rural areas, sugar planters accommodated this marked rise in the number of youths.[7] They provided recreational activities for both boys and girls on the plantations and did their best to circumvent any social disruption that could be caused by an uneven sex ratio. Planters sought to avoid large-scale strikes like those of 1909, 1920, and 1924—strikes made possible, in some part, to a small degree of cooperation between Japanese and Filipino workers against a common adversary, their planter employers.[8] By the end of the nineteenth century planters had consciously developed a system of labor recruitment that sought to pit the racial antagonisms of one ethnic immigrant group against another.[9] But even in these years the seeds of interethnic cooperation and communication had been planted. Jonathan Okamura traces the beginnings of a local identity to a basic tension rooted in the plantation experience: "Viewed historically, the emergence of local culture and society represents an accommodation of ethnic groups to one another in the context of a social system primarily distinguished by the wide cleavage between the Haole planter and merchant oligarchy on the one hand, and the subordinate [Native] Hawaiians and immigrant plantation groups on the other."[10]

Local culture and society emerged in Hawai'i as a direct response to the hegemonic control exerted by a white elite: local identity was an identity formed in opposition. The mixing of disparate ethnic cultures and the sharing of a new, hybrid culture also contributed to the development of this local identity. And yet there was always room for intralocal conflict; Okamura warns against a naive conception of local culture that paints Hawai'i as a "'laboratory of race relations' where peoples of sharply differing traditions are able to live in harmony with one another."[11]

Though a basic tension between whites and nonwhites lay at the core of local culture, the plantation system itself did little to encourage solidarity between different ethnic groups: these groups "were housed in segregated camps, received differential wages for the same work, held differential access to skilled positions, and were imported as strikebreakers against one another."[12] But the plantation experience did give rise to pidgin, or Hawai'i Creole English (HCE)—a language born of struggle and the hardships of plantation life that was shared by all ethnic laborer groups. Although this common language could not unite workers in all instances, it was one that allowed them to communicate with one another and was passed on to their children.[13]

In the city of Honolulu the children and grandchildren of plantation workers used HCE in their neighborhoods and schools. It did not necessarily prevent ethnic differences among young men and women, but it was nevertheless a shared language of members of the working class. The second- and third-generation children of immigrants with whom Ben Ahakuelo cavorted around town were definitely pidgin speakers. Though sometimes knowledgeable about their parents' native Japanese, Cantonese, Ilocano, Visayan, or, in Ben's case, Hawaiian, their primary language outside the home was usually a variant of English. Often the English was "not the language of Shakespeare,"[14] since the majority of these children of working-class backgrounds were not admitted to English Standard public schools like Roosevelt High School or the private Punahou and St. Louis schools, which prided themselves in teaching Standard English. The pidgin spoken by these generations was a modified form of the makeshift language spoken on the plantations, but one that linguist John Reinecke would call a "true local Hawaiian Island dialect of American English" nonetheless.[15] Transformed in the schools and on the streets, the pidgin of Honolulu served as a common language as well. According to Reinecke, a new, colonial dialect of pidgin spoken in the city tended to outlive the creole dialect spoken on the plantations. As the plantation economy began to decrease in importance, so too did the old creole dialect of pidgin.[16]

The colonial dialect of HCE served as a common language in the schools and neighborhoods of Honolulu in much the same way that the creole dialect had served as a mode of communication on rural plantations. Ben Ahakuelo had known Henry Chang, Joseph Kahahawai, Horace Ida, and David Takai since his early youth, and all five used the colonial dialect of HCE, since it was the lingua franca of their neighborhood. They lived within a one-mile radius of the home of Sylvester P. Correa—where they visited on the night of Saturday, September 12, 1931, to attend a luau.[17] If we are to believe the observations of the missionary Mrs. Tyssowski, all five knew each other well enough to form a gang known as the Kauluwela Gang. At the very least, we can be certain that they all attended Kauluwela School together during 1920–1924.

Most of what we know about the Kauluwela Boys comes from courtroom and police interrogation room testimony and the observations of others recorded in the Pinkerton reports. The young men themselves offer little testimony outside the official queries by the Honolulu police and legal system. In fact, it was not until 1968 that one of the suspects, Ben Ahakuelo, granted an interview with a newspaper reporter about the Massie case.[18] In the absence of documents written by the Kauluwela Boys, a strategic reading of court and police sources reveals social groupings, dates, times, and other details that can be corroborated with other evidence. These sources have also captured the use of HCE by local youths. In transcribing the dialogue between officials (speakers of Standard English) and local youths (speakers of HCE), the bias was clearly on the side of officials recording the testimony. Even though the words of local youths were recorded with such bias, it can be read as a marker of a linguistic boundary that separated those in power from those without.

THE SCHOOL GROUND AS A SITE OF RECREATION AND INVESTIGATION

Police and representatives of the court were not the only officials to record the language of local youths. Educators interacted with these youths on a daily basis in less sensationalistic circumstances and have provided a plethora of information about their local charges. They witnessed how children of varying ethnic backgrounds were brought into close proximity to one another in classrooms and schoolyards. Local identity was formed in these common spaces. In response to the spread of Pidgin English, a number of haole parents sought to separate their children from non-haoles by pushing for the establishment of English Standard schools.

In both the English Standard and non-Standard schools, whites made up the majority of the faculty.[19] Their attitudes toward their students ranged considerably, but as teachers, all were careful observers who had daily interactions with local youths. Mrs. Tyssowski, for example, knew the Kauluwela Boys from an early age and considered herself to be well aware of the social circles in which they congregated. In her remarks to a Pinkerton investigator, she showed her skills as a social observer:

Henry [Chang] for a while seemed to be going all right although he still ran with the Vineyard St. Gang, who all formed a class taught by [a] missionary's wife. In this class were Joe Kahahawai (alias Kalani), Ben Ahakuelo, [Horace] Ida (for a little while), [and David] Takai (occasionally). The club work [at the school] seemed to be a meeting place for the gang; it cemented it together. I often heard of what the Kakaako gang, Palama gang, Kalihi gang and what they (the KAULUWELA gang) were going to do to the others. They all lived in that vicinity, just off Vineyard Street.[20]

In this selection, Tyssowski reveals that local youths like the Kauluwela Boys were able to make the most of their situations. She admitted that instead of succumbing entirely to their teacher's efforts, the boys (aged thirteen or fifteen in 1924) used the mission itself as their own "meeting place for the gang." Local culture emerged in the 1930s, drawing upon dominant American institutions and appropriating selected elements of popular culture chosen by local youths according to their own desires and ends. Schools and missionary activities brought individuals of varying ethnic backgrounds together. But even at a young age the Kauluwela Boys knew how to turn the tables on authority figures like their teachers and do things on their own terms. In Sunday school, for example, Horace Ida found a way to make trouble. As one missionary observed, "[The] Missionary's wife in telling of Virgin Birth at Xmas first got very well acquainted with Ida, who was sitting in back seats nudging boys and smiling, making slurring remarks during her talk. He was rebuked; and later Mr. Tyssowski had to put him entirely out of [the] club, due to his profane language in the midst of games. He then took great delight in being [a] leader of boys and trying to pull them out of Sunday School."[21]

Acting up in class was only one minor form of rebellion. More important were the variety of recreational activities that local youths participated in for their own enjoyment. Dominant American culture offered football, boxing, and baseball; media including radio and movies; and social dances in large public spaces where young men and women of various backgrounds could mingle.[22] To date, the role of American culture in the development of local culture in Hawai'i has not been explored. Instead, scholars of Hawai'i have often cast American culture and institutions as taking part in a larger Americanization process that was for the most part destructive to older immigrant cultures.[23]

Specifically, these young men's physical activities gained them both notoriety and suspicion. Ben Ahakuelo, for example, was a well-known athlete in
the community. He had represented the Territory of Hawaiʻi in the Amateur
Athletic Union (AAU) boxing championships at Madison Square Garden in
April 1931, and with a pending reprieve by Governor Judd he hoped to represent the territory again in the welterweight division in 1932. However, due
to the national coverage of the Massie case, Ahakuelo's coach feared for his
safety in New York City, and he never made the trip in 1932.[24] Like his best
friend Joseph Kahahawai, also an amateur boxer, Ahakuelo starred in neighborhood barefoot football games on Sunday afternoons. Newspapers on the
continental United States often cast Ahakuelo and Kahahawai as "hoodlums"
who might use their physical prowess in sports to fight white servicemen or
assault women, white or otherwise.

In portraying these two Native Hawaiians as "savage brutes," newspapers
and true-crime magazines on the continent suggested that Ahakuelo and
Kahahawai were hulking figures. Yet as members of a 150-pound football
league, both young men were lighter than most servicemen stationed on
Oʻahu. In fact, many local young men pointed out their small to medium
builds when stopped by police for scuffles with servicemen. In order to quell
mainland fears, police officials themselves also made this difference in physical size clear in their reports. One year after the Massie case, for example,
Chief Charles F. Weeber of the Honolulu Police Department wrote a memorandum for Governor Judd and Secretary of the Interior Ray Lyman Wilbur
detailing a small altercation between two army officers and three civilians.
Both officers in this fight were "large men" while all three of the civilians were
"of slight build and small stature" ranging from 140 to 158 pounds.[25]

To say the least, tensions between the local youth population and servicemen had been growing since World War I and the arrival of the fleet in
1925.[26] Recreational activities such as sports events and dances, as well as other popular amusements, were most often the sites for such conflicts between
local male youths and servicemen. Sports promoters recognized that such
tension could work to their advantage, so they used the basic rivalry between
local young men and servicemen in order to draw larger crowds at football
games and boxing matches.[27]

For the most part, however, local youths and servicemen did their best to
keep interactions to a minimum. They kept separate social circles, especially
in the arena of social amusements. On the weekend of September 12–13,

1931, two different celebrations were in progress: Thomas and Thalia Massie attended a "tea party"—a euphemism for a drinking party—at the Ala Wai Inn, a Japanese tea house in Waikīkī overlooking the Ala Wai canal, while in another part of town the Kauluwela Boys attended a luau and later ended up at a dance at the Aloha Amusement Park. Both celebrations took place in Waikīkī—an area that was (and still is) a place for lively evenings for locals, servicemen, and tourists. Before we turn to the events that brought Thalia Massie and the Kauluwela Boys within a half-mile of each other on the night of September 12 and the early hours of September 13, it is necessary to view the separate parties earlier in the evening. The gathering of each set of individuals in two different parts of town highlights the division between locals and nonlocals.

THE CULTURAL GEOGRAPHY OF URBAN HONOLULU

Local consciousness and identity were formed along lines of geographic opposition. National media contrasted conditions in Hawai'i with those on the U.S. continent. Closer to home, the day-to-day social interactions and boundaries found in the islands were more immediate to the formation of local identity for boys like Ben Ahakuelo and his friends. On the island of O'ahu, where the events of the Massie case took place, there was a clear division between the residences of the haves and the have-nots.[28] A strict separation between urban and rural areas was never fully achieved, but exclusive residences did exist by the 1930s. The city of Honolulu was a diverse one, indeed, split into working-class neighborhoods, light industrial districts, wet farmlands, and comfortable suburban areas. In 1930 University of Hawai'i sociologist Andrew Lind found the city of Honolulu diverse enough to map its areas of social disorganization.

According to Lind, delinquency and disorganization in Honolulu tended to follow "the same spatial patterns as in other cities," albeit with some variations caused by cultural differences among ethnic groups.[29] Lind's study shows a slight proclivity of sociologists to blame juveniles for crime, but it is generally sympathetic to the viewpoints of the youths themselves. His study is also an excellent source in describing the geography of Honolulu almost precisely at the moment of the Massie case. In fact, Lind found it necessary in his article to point to the recent uproar in the island press over what it perceived to be a crime wave shortly before the Massie case: "The community of Honolulu, including its resort population, has recently been greatly exercised over a series of crimes, each of which has been embellished and emphasized by the local press. The Fukunaga kidnapping and murder case [of 1928–1929], a group of subsequent crimes involving members of one of the racial groups least given to delinquent behavior, and a number of recent sex offenses have served to focus general attention upon the alleged Hawaiian 'crime wave.'"[30]

In the city of Honolulu, large mountain ridges extend to the ocean, serving to break the city into a number of pie-shaped valleys. In precontact times all of the islands were split into *moku,* and these *moku* were split into smaller *ahupua'a*—geographic districts that were individually self-sufficient.[31] By the twentieth century these *ahupua'a* did not function in the way that they had before, but they still lent their names to many of the valleys in the Hawaiian Islands. The valleys central to this study are Mānoa and the Kalihi-Pālama areas.

Honolulu had problems comparable to American cities of its size, with some geographic differences due to its mountain ranges created by volcanic activity. This unique topography altered the geographic distribution of the population in Honolulu, but for the most part patterns of organization and disorganization tended to follow those of other cities. Lind found a high concentration of cases of juvenile delinquency, family dependency, suicides, and common vice in two areas, Pālama and Kaka'ako. Located just outside the business district of Honolulu, these were "areas of transition between residence and business, of high value and low residential rents, characteristic of all cities."[32] Kalihi also showed a high rate of disorganization. It had been an area of early residential settlement, but was showing signs of industrial invasion by the early 1930s and hence decreasing residential value. There was no clear border between Kalihi and Pālama; residents in the vicinity often referred to the area as Kalihi-Pālama, or Kapālama.

KALIHI-PĀLAMA: A PLACE OF TRANSITION

Honolulu's working classes lived in these areas of greatest "social disorganization." The young working-class men accused of raping Thalia Massie lived in the Kalihi-Pālama area and their social experiences stood in contrast to those of the Massie party, who resided in Mānoa, a residential section of Honolulu.

A scant four miles separated the homes of the defendants on or near Frog Lane and the Massies on Kahawai Street and Grace Fortescue on Kolowalu Street. As in other major cities on the continental United States, rich and poor could live in close proximity to one another and yet lead totally different lives. For Ben Ahakuelo, Henry Chang, and the other men accused of rape in 1931, place of residence had much to do with whom they socialized with around town. All five of the young men attended Kauluwela School and were known at that time as the Kauluwela Gang. In this case the word "gang" simply indicated a group of friends, and a person from one gang could certainly hang out with another gang from time to time. Such gangs did not have exclusive membership, nor were they organized necessarily for the purpose of committing crimes.[33] As the remarks by Mrs. Tyssowski earlier suggest, this group of boys was not unlike the Vineyard Street Gang, Kakaʻako Gang, Pālama Gang, Kalihi Gang, and others that were named after the streets or geographic areas where the boys lived and congregated together. Except for Kahahawai, who was lucky enough to attend the private St. Louis School, the boys attended the non–English Standard McKinley High School. Though their high schools separated them during the morning hours of the week, the boys maintained their friendship through participation in sports in the afternoons and on weekends.

ACTIVITIES AND MOVEMENT: "GANGS" AND RECREATION

Though the press, government officials, and the police often criminalized local male youths, the exhaustive Richardson Report, undertaken at the behest of the Department of the Interior, found that there was "no organized crime element" in the islands of any sort. The federal report recognized that there were slight incidences of juvenile delinquency in Honolulu, but at a rate no higher than other comparably sized cities on the U.S. continent. Given the high rate of unemployment in Honolulu during this period, some territorial and federal officials were surprised that there was not a great deal of crime. Instead of coming together to commit crimes, young local males gathered because of the bonds they had developed through school, sports, or place of residence. All three of these elements overlapped with one another: place of residence determined the public school one attended, and school or neighborhood playground determined the sports teams one joined.

In the case of the Kauluwela Boys, all five attended the same elementary school and played football in Honolulu's barefoot football league. They all practiced at Kauluwela field behind the school at one time or another, since it was a popular field for barefoot football practices and games. As schoolchildren they had rivalries with the teams of different neighborhoods, but they hardly produced any lasting social divisions among working-class boys who would eventually become working-class men. If anything, participation in sports served to reinforce solidarity among locals by introducing them to individuals with similar backgrounds from their own neighborhoods as well as from other parts of the city. As Kalihi resident Peter Martin would later recall of his sporting activities, "That's how we get to know the people."[34] When asked if he fought with members of rival football teams, Martin demonstrated bonds of sociability, linking himself with other working-class youths. He had nothing against similar boys from Kaka'ako, for example, though they were the greatest rivals of Kalihi boys: "I never did get in trouble over there [in Kaka'ako]. No kidding. I get to know all of them, too. You know, from playing other sports beside only football. I played softball, I get to meet them. And we can sit down. Maybe someplace, we drinking, all da kine, talk stories, but no fight."[35] When there was fighting it was usually contained, remarked Martin, who played football against the likes of Ben Ahakuelo from 1922 to 1930: "And before, those days, way back, when you fight, you stand up and fight. No more the gang stuff. If he lick you, then you two guys shake hands. *Pau* [finished], go your way. [Chuckles] Not later on. Not like now days." Martin explained that a "bull"—a leader—was the one who held sway over an area, called the shots, and limited any sort of fighting: "That's why, way back before, nearly every district, they had their own 'bull,' they call 'em—the head man, eh?"[36]

A certain measure of physical strength was needed in order to grow up as a local boy in these working-class neighborhoods. Knowing how to box had its advantages. Martin and others like him knew this well: "I was no troublemaker. But once in a while I used to get fights, though. The guys who used to pick on me, well, up and up. Before, I used to take up boxing, too, see? So, I know [a] little about fighting. So, I used to take care of myself. But I'm not the kind of bully guy go look for trouble or what. Well, most of the guys in Kalihi, they know me so they no bother."[37]

It was no easy task to grow up in Kalihi-Pālama, or any other of the nearby working-class neighborhoods of Honolulu. The sports activities of the Kaluwela Boys legitimated them as part of a male local youth culture and brought them into contact with youths of other working-class neighborhoods as well. The geography of the city also reveals zones of compatibility and competition: within one's own neighborhood, there was a palpable sense of belonging—of being linked to a place. In Honolulu, the place one called "home" marked the enclave that was to be most protected. And yet when one went beyond the limits of his home neighborhood, he approached a kind of danger. Daily activities of work and play brought individuals into different sectors of the city, and hence into zones of potential conflict. In these instances, individuals like the Kaluwela Boys transgressed both physical and social boundaries—even when traveling only a short distance. By crossing into a different space, boys moved into a new geographic and, therefore, new social world where they risked being alienated or even hurt.

Making the distinction here between "place" and "space" allows us to be more precise about the relationship between identity and movement.[38] "Place" denotes a geographic site with a known history that allows individuals to form a bond with that particular geography; "space" is a more neutral term that often refers to an area or distance (whether social or physical) that is momentarily inhabited or transgressed.[39] One could certainly affirm one's identity by linking it to a place, but could also affirm other aspects of identity through the daily social activities that required movement beyond home and into less familiar spaces. In the case of Peter Martin and the Kaluwela Boys, sports brought them into contact with other boys from nearby working-class neighborhoods. Elements of danger were sometimes present—the possibility of a sports rivalry breaking out into a brawl, for example—but these sorts of dangers were muted by a feeling of common ground. Boys from Kalihi might not be the best of friends with those of nearby Iwilei, but they certainly had points of compatibility: they shared a sense of what it meant to be a young man interested in sports, and all were members of the working class during the Depression and young adults negotiating the differences between their ethnic upbringing and their Americanized social activities.

Kalihi-Pālama, Iwilei, and Kaka'ako—three sectors of Honolulu identified by Lind as areas of "social disorganization"—were united by their working-class status and their proximity to one another. All areas had the same level of household income despite their varying ethnic compositions: Iwilei was largely inhabited by Portuguese[40] and Native Hawaiians; Kaka'ako had a high percentage of Japanese; Kalihi-Pālama was home to a mix of Chinese,

Filipinos, Portuguese, and Native Hawaiians.[41] None of these areas was ever considered the domain of whites.[42]

Danger existed most likely whenever individuals crossed a great distance, both social and physical, and moved into a space that was open to more than one demographic group. This was the case on the night of September 12–13, 1931, when the Kauluwela Boys traveled to Waikīkī for a night on the town. Waikīkī was the playground for a variety of different social groups and was also home to some, but the area discussed here functioned in the same way that the Luna Park amusement area did for New York.[43] Honolulu, like other American cities, had its areas for working-class recreation. By returning to the events of that night in September, we shall see how the Kauluwela Boys entered the danger zone.

SATURDAY NIGHT, SEPTEMBER 12, 1931: BOYS ON THE TOWN

The evening of revelry began at the boys' homes in Kalihi-Pālama. Horace Ida borrowed his sister's car for the evening and intended to put it to good use. In search of drink during this age of Prohibition, he stopped first at the Mochizuki Tea House and later a Filipino speakeasy. There he ran into his fellow Japanese friends David Takai and "Buster" Seki. Ben Ahakuelo, a Native Hawaiian and friend from their neighborhood and the football league, soon joined them for a few beers. Ahakuelo knew that another neighbor, Sylvester P. Correa, was having a luau to celebrate the marriage of his daughter Beatrice. As a supervisor of the City and County of Honolulu, Correa could be expected to throw a large party.[44]

Ida, Takai, Ahakuelo, and Seki were friends with Correa's son, "Doc," and knew they could count on at least a few beers. The four decided to enjoy the party outdoors, since they had not been formally invited. When the party quieted a bit, they decided to go to the Aloha Amusement Park in Waikīkī, where locals could always look forward to a Saturday night dance. Takai and Ahakuelo were more enthusiastic about the dance than Ida and Seki, so Ida dropped them off at the amusement park and planned to do a bit of touring in his sister's car.[45]

Ida and Ahakuelo eventually ended up back at the Correa luau, where they ran into two more friends, both of Native Hawaiian descent: Joseph

Kahahawai was a full-blooded Hawaiian (and, like Ahakuelo, a well-known football and boxing champion), and Henry Chang was of Hawaiian-Chinese ancestry. The four eventually decided that the dance at the Aloha Amusement Park was their best bet for entertainment that night, so they set out for Waikīkī.

It was 11:30 p.m. by the time they arrived at the park, and the dance ended at midnight. Ahakuelo went ahead in order to enter the park in time. Kahahawai and Chang lingered in the parking lot for a while; then, thinking it would not be worth paying admission by that point, Chang obtained a couple of ticket stubs from his friend, John Puaaloa, who was leaving the dance to take his date home. Chang and Kahahawai were now able to enter the dance—and at no cost. Once in the park, they met up again with Ahakuelo and Takai, thus making the Kauluwela Boys almost complete as a group. Ida was still hanging out in the parking lot; the four assembled thought it unfair that the driver should not enjoy at least some of the fun, so Kahahawai elected to go outside for a while so that Ida could use his ticket stub to enter the dance.

By this point it was almost midnight, and people were leaving. Ida, not ready for the night to end, decided that the group should leave and see if the Correa luau was still in progress. By law the music was supposed to stop at midnight, but it was not until 12:05 a.m. that the dance band stopped playing. At that point all five of the Kauluwela Boys—Ida, Ahakuelo, Chang, Takai, and Kahahawai—exited into the parking lot and piled into the car, Ida at the wheel. Chang and Kahahawai, in blue jeans and white silk shirts, were in keeping with the fashion of working-class youths. Ida wore a leather jacket.[46]

Heading home to Kalihi-Pālama would prove to be more exciting than the luau they planned to return to. Ida went *mauka* (toward the mountains) on Kalākaua Avenue.[47] According to his recollection, he drove along a new extension of Kalākaua Avenue that allowed him to turn left onto Beretania Street.[48] He was following a car driven by Tatsumi "Tuts" Matsumoto that carried Margaret Kanae, Sybil Davis, George Silva, and Robert Vierra. As the two cars traveled along Beretania in the ʻewa direction (roughly west, toward ʻEwa Beach), they approached Linekona School and Thomas Square. The cars were side by side when they passed the Honolulu Academy of Arts building. Vierra instructed Matsumoto to drive the car at the same speed as Ida's because Ahakuelo appeared to want to ask him (Vierra) a question. Vierra daringly stepped across to the running board of Ida's car while both

cars were in motion, moving down Beretania Street. Ahakuelo asked where
Matsumoto and his group were going; Vierra responded that they were headed toward Judd Street.[49]

   After this bit of excitement, there was nothing left for the boys but to see
if the Correa luau was still on. When they arrived, most of the guests had
already left, although someone was still playing music. According to later
testimony by Chang, the party was winding down, and the few remaining
guests were singing "Memories." Ahakuelo lived nearby, so after asking Doc
Correa if there was any beer left and finding that there was none, he walked
home. He did, after all, have football practice in the morning, so as far as he
was concerned, the evening was over. Ida also decided to call it a night and
drive Kahahawai, Takai, and Chang back to their homes.

SUNDAY, SEPTEMBER 13, 1931

When the Honolulu police approached Ahakuelo during football practice
early Sunday afternoon, he had little idea why he would be questioned. He
had been in trouble with the law before, but this time he saw no reason for
immediate alarm.[50] He soon learned, however, that the police had picked up
his friends Kahahawai, Takai, and Chang at their homes earlier in the day.

   Ida was the first of the five Kauluwela Boys to be questioned: Officers
Cluney and Black arrived at his home at 2:50 a.m., having received a com-
plaint from Mrs. Agnes Peeples that the Ford touring car he was driving had
nearly hit her and her husband at the intersection of King and Liliha Streets.
Since the 1929 Ford Phaeton was registered to his sister, Ida at first tried to
deny that he had been in any trouble earlier that night. He was no doubt tired
from chauffeuring his friends around town all night. When the Correa luau
had finally come to an end, all that was left for Ida to do was drive Takai,
Chang, and Kahahawai home. He never expected to get into a minor traffic
accident at King and Liliha Streets. Out of embarrassment he initially tried to
cover up what had happened to protect his friend, Kahahawai: when a Hud-
son driven by Mr. Homer Peeples had nearly hit them, Kahahawai jumped
out of the car and allegedly yelled, "Get that goddamn haole out of the car and
I'll give him what he's looking for!"[51] Mrs. Peeples, a large Hawaiian woman,
got out of the car but left her smaller white husband at the wheel. She pushed
Kahahawai and he responded by punching her in the mouth. When Mr. Peeples began searching for the tire iron in his car, Kahahawai and his friends

jumped back into the Ford Phaeton and sped away. Mrs. Peeples, however, had recovered enough to memorize its license-plate number: 58-895.

Police radios all over Honolulu began broadcasting the license number after 1:00 a.m., and in the estimation of author Theon Wright, it was quite possible that shortly after 3:00 a.m. the number was "repeated several times in the presence of Lieutenant Massie and other Navy personnel" at Queen's Hospital, where Thalia Massie was being treated.[52] By 3:30 a.m. Thalia had arrived at the police station to speak with Inspector McIntosh and was able to provide him with a license number of the car in which she believed she had been abducted: "I think it was 58-805. I would not swear to that being correct. I just caught a fleeting glimpse of it as they drove away."[53]

The fact that the two license numbers differed by a single digit seemed to connect the Kauluwela Boys to the rape of Thalia Massie. But if we look instead at the testimony of Ahakuelo in 1968, we see a different interpretation of why he and his friends were singled out in 1931: "We got picked up because we were wild kids and they had to have somebody and they got the orders from up top to get someone and so we were it. We were wild kids fighting in the streets and going to dance halls but we weren't the right guys who raped Mrs. Massie."[54] In addition to asserting the innocence of himself and his friends, Ahakuelo cast himself as part of a group that stood in opposition to authority figures "up top." As "wild kids fighting in the streets and going to dance halls," Ahakuelo and other young men like him represented a threat to the social order of urban Honolulu.[55] From the standpoint of local youths, the Kauluwela Boys were simply young men enjoying a night on the town that evening. To others, however, they had possibly committed a wrong by traveling beyond the boundary of their local working-class neighborhood and into a zone that whites also used for recreation. As we shall see in the next chapter, officials were already trying to build a case that would link local young men to the assault of a white woman in Ala Moana that evening. By Monday morning the press had caught wind of the story and branded these newly accused young men the "Ala Moana Boys."[56]

2

....

Thalia Massie
and the Defense of
White Womanhood

A car drove up behind me and stopped. Two men got off the car
and grabbed me and dragged me into their car. One of them placed
a hand over my mouth. When they got me into the back seat of
the car they held me down between them. They were Hawaiians. I
begged and pleaded with them to let me go. . . . They drove the car
into the undergrowth on the right-hand side of [Ala Moana Road],
dragged me out and away from the car into the bushes and assaulted me. I was assaulted six or seven times.

—*Testimony of Thalia Massie to Inspector John McIntosh of the Honolulu
Police Department,* SEPTEMBER 13, 1931, HONOLULU, HAWAI'I[1]

THALIA MASSIE HAD marks on her body to indicate that she had been the
victim of a very violent crime. The fact that she was a white woman and
that her alleged assailants were a group of nonwhite men gave her story in-
credible strength. Several people have asserted that Thalia Massie was never
raped. While I use the term "alleged rape" in this chapter, it is by no means
an attempt to deny the seriousness of her charges. Rather, I use the term to

counter the dominant discourse of the 1930s that automatically assumed a rape had occurred and that the Kaluwela Boys, as young men of color, had no doubt committed the crime. I do not scrutinize Massie's story in order to determine whether or not the Kaluwela Boys indeed raped her on the night of September 12, 1931; we are not likely to resolve this question any more clearly than the detectives, jurors, and thousands of readers who followed the Ala Moana assault trial in the early 1930s. Instead, what we can do is examine how Massie's story of being a white woman raped by nonwhite men contributed to the formation of local identity in Hawai'i by reaffirming a larger pattern of haole dominance that separated whites from nonwhites along lines of race and gender. Her story of rape illustrated and maintained a racialized and gendered boundary between white women and men of color that was crucial to the formation of local identity in Hawai'i.

Thalia Massie's story was more than just a personal narrative of tragedy. It became more than her own and served as a powerful rallying force for the haole community in Honolulu in the early 1930s. Stories about the suffering of white women have historically mobilized communities that imagine themselves as subject to adverse new environments and conditions. In early America, for example, the captivity narrative of Mary Rowlandson was a powerful one of a white woman captured by "Indian savages." Rowlandson and other women captured by Native Americans in the seventeenth, eighteenth, and nineteenth centuries were like Thalia Massie in that they saw themselves as victims at the hands of nonwhite men in the wilderness. Unlike Massie, however, most women who told such "Indian" captivity narratives denied that they were sexually assaulted. Rowlandson said that when she was taken captive in 1676, she had been forced to sleep "in the midst of those roaring lions and savage bears that feared neither God nor man nor the devil" but that none of her captors "ever offered the least abuse of unchastity to me in word or action."[2] Whether these accounts were credible or were edited for modesty, these early captivity narratives were markedly different from Massie's story of rape. During the Ala Moana assault trial she testified that she was sexually assaulted five or six times, that her assailants "talked to each other in some foreign language," and that when they spoke in English, "they said a lot of filthy things to me."[3]

The narratives of Mary Rowlandson and Thalia Massie were similar, however, in that they rallied white men to act in defense of white women. Susan Brownmiller notes that especially during Western expansion in the

nineteenth century, "white men talked freely at the time of the rape of white
women—and often used these stories as an inflammatory excuse for their
own behavior." Brownmiller believes that during Rowlandson's time and the
nineteenth century, women were comparatively reluctant to use stories of
rape as rationales for violence.[4] In 1930s Honolulu women did not advocate
vigilantism either, but they were more likely to participate in organizations
that would prevent future sexual assaults.

Communities on the continent and in Hawai'i saw Thalia Massie's assault
as a flagrant sexual transgression of the color line that needed to be addressed
quickly. To say that the story of her rape articulated a boundary means that
the narrative of her tragedy was both an expression of white anxiety about
interracial contact in Hawai'i and a linking of these fears in the islands to a
larger patriarchal system of terror that separated men of color from white
women on the continental United States.[5]

Massie's narrative of rape was thus both a local story and a national one.
Wherever white American women lived, a white system of law was expected
to prevail. Admiral William Pratt, the Chief of Naval Operations for the U.S.
Navy at the time, spoke out about the case and declared, "American men will
not stand for the violation of their women under any circumstances."[6] As
the Scottsboro case and numerous other incidents in the American South
indicated, merely the charge of raping a white woman was enough to speed
nonwhite male suspects to trial and encourage a conviction. Whenever men
of color seemed to cross the line and made advances toward white women, a
system of white patriarchal power could quickly combine legal and extralegal
measures to enforce the boundary once again. For example, white men like
Rear Admiral Yates Stirling Jr., who at the time was commandant of the 14th
Naval District, Pearl Harbor, could not see the alleged rape of Massie "as a
mere miscarriage of justice which has happened in many communities on the
mainland." In Stirling's estimation the Massie case had "lessened the prestige
of white peoples the world over, where-ever [sic] they are in contact with the
darker skinned people."[7]

Massie's story had the backing of multiple communities—women's
groups in Hawai'i, the haole oligarchy, and the continental U.S.—that had
generated a racial hierarchy of white over black. The patriarchal and racialized ideology that aimed to keep nonwhite men away from white women
brought the full force of a continent to bear on the culturally different place of
Hawai'i. Local identity was formed in opposition to this dominant ideology,

and its development also depended on the spatial dimensions of Honolulu. Geographic segregation was an intentional way to separate white communities from their nonwhite counterparts. The differences between Mānoa and working-class neighborhoods like Kalihi-Pālama showed locals that their way of life was much different from those of the haole community. The remarks of continental Americans during the Massie case also indicated to locals that people on the "Mainland" found them to be quite different from citizens on the continent. The cultural and racial differences of locals and their geographic distance from the continental United States made them seem like second-class citizens at best and "un-American" at worst. Continental Americans depended largely on print media and other institutions available to them in assessing Hawai'i, the Massie case, and Thalia Massie's story of rape. Benedict Anderson has argued that three institutions of power—the census, the map, and the museum—have often come together and "profoundly shaped the way in which the colonial state imagined its dominion— the nature of the human beings it ruled, the geography of its domain, and the legitimacy of its ancestry."[8] In the case of Hawai'i, an outpost far from the continental U.S., the fate of island residents often rested in the whims and imaginations of those on the continent.

CRIES OF RAPE: WHOSE VOICE? WHOSE AGENCY?

Thalia Massie identified the Kauluwela Boys as her assailants and eventually testified against them in the Ala Moana assault trial of November 1931. In this respect, she exhibited her agency and a power of voice heard publicly to a degree perhaps unusual for most rape victims. Feminist scholars have pointed to the inherent difficulties faced by claimants of rape: they face a legal system that is structured to deny their claim and places the burden on them to prove that they are victims of a sexual assault.[9] Massie experienced some of these difficulties, but she also had status as a white woman in a place largely considered a colonial outpost of the United States.[10] Her personal voice and personal story of rape were elevated by the fact that she was white, a woman of social standing, and the wife of a naval officer.

Her words to the police, her testimony on the stand, and her occasional remarks to reporters were printed on the front pages of local and national papers. Had Massie not been a white woman of high social stature, the press would not have given her such a public voice. Had her alleged assailants been white, her rape likely would not have received the same degree of coverage by the general press in Hawai'i, nor would her story have made the national news.

The Japanese American press was often critical of establishment newspapers such as the *Honolulu Advertiser* and *Honolulu Star-Bulletin*. The Japanese and English-language newspaper *Jitsugyo-no-Hawaii* characterized the early months of 1932 as a period of white hysteria. In January 1932 two events stirred the haole community: on January 2 Mrs. James Odowda, a white woman, was allegedly raped in her Wilhelmina Rise home by escaped convict Lui Kaikapu, a Native Hawaiian man.

Less than a week later one white woman and three white men were arrested by the Honolulu Police Department: Thalia Massie's mother, Grace Fortescue; Thalia's husband, Thomas Massie; and enlisted sailors Albert Jones and Edward Lord. All were accused of killing Joseph Kahahawai on January 8 in retaliation for his alleged role in the rape of Thalia Massie. The *Jitsugyo-no-Hawaii* saw these events as "a few sporadic crimes that followed each other in such rapid succession."[11] Instead of characterizing early January as a crime wave, like the *Honolulu Advertiser* had done, the *Jitsugyo-no-Hawaii* believed that Honolulu was the same as it had always been except for "a certain white element of the city who lost their sanity." Unlike the mainstream *Advertiser* and *Star-Bulletin,* the Japanese American paper identified race as the crucial difference: "It might have been a far different story had the unfortunate victims in the Ala Moana and the Wilhelmina Rise cases been other than haoles."[12]

Locals drew attention to the fact that women of color who were the victims of rape in Hawai'i did not have the same power as that of Thalia Massie's public voice. The *Jitsugyo-no-Hawaii* complained that when a Japanese matron was raped in February 1932 near what was then known as John Rodgers Airport, there was not a "ripple of excitement" among other papers "other than a passing remark that another woman had been raped."[13] By comparison, the white community in Hawai'i was outraged whenever crimes against white women were reported, and the *Honolulu Advertiser* frequently afforded these stories ample coverage.

Thalia Massie's voice was heard often during the case and her statements are faithfully recorded in police testimony and trial transcripts. Her words are also easily accessible in two early accounts of the Massie case, Theon Wright's

Rape in Paradise (1966) and Peter Van Slingerland's *Something Terrible Has Happened* (1966). The titles of these books emphasize that the principal crime was one of sexual transgression. But Massie's story was about much more than rape; it was also about the distribution of power in the Territory of Hawai'i and the relationship of the territory to the continental United States. Newspaper accounts, civic groups, territorial officials, the Chamber of Commerce, and the Big Five firms (Alexander & Baldwin, American Factors, Castle and Cooke, C. Brewer, and Theo Davies) all utilized Massie's story of rape to their own ends.

The Big Five planter and merchant elites saw Massie's story as a way to generate support from across the nation in defense of white womanhood. Her story was also employed to rally for the preservation of haole privilege in Hawai'i. The haole elite were effectively an oligarchy, holding power over an entire set of islands. In less than a century this small group had carved out a space for themselves in government, agriculture, and business. In press accounts both in Hawai'i and on the continent, readers were assured that despite the majority of the population being nonwhite Native Hawaiians, Asians, and others, Hawai'i and specifically Honolulu were places where "The White Man's Manner of Life Prevails."[14]

Since the 1870s the military had also been one of the first official presences of the United States in Hawai'i, following American businessmen and missionaries. In Hawai'i locals witnessed an increase in military personnel and equipment in the early twentieth century as the United States readied itself for two world wars. The island of O'ahu, home to Pearl Harbor and the city of Honolulu, the seat of territorial government and center of business, was home to a majority of the territory's population by 1930. As a central point of the territory, 87 percent of the white population lived there.[15] This presence and preservation of white privilege in Hawai'i was etched into the landscape of Honolulu itself.

PATTERNS OF HAOLE DOMINANCE:
WHITENESS ON THE CONTINENT
AND IN HAWAI'I

The word "haole" is often used to denote "whites" in Hawai'i, but the word in its earliest usage described any foreigners or non-Native Hawaiians in the islands. The exact etymology is not known, but several have suggested that it perhaps comes from the combination of "ha" and "ole," meaning "without breath," or without the ability to speak Hawaiian.[16] By the end of the nine-teenth century the term was limited almost solely to whites in the islands. Whites from the United States, Great Britain, and other countries have a long history in Hawai'i, and it would be incorrect to gather all of these experiences under the rubric of "white" or haole. But by the early twentieth century the term was used mostly in reference to whites from the United States, either those who had become entrenched in the Territory of Hawai'i over genera-tions or the newly arrived servicemen and their families.[17] Like David Stan-nard, Ronald Takaki, Gary Okihiro, Judy Rohrer, and other scholars of Ha-wai'i, I use the term "haole" because of its historical specificity and accepted usage in the islands.[18]

The haole oligarchy had been in the making for some time before the arrival of Thalia and Thomas Massie.[19] Lawrence Fuchs, a noted historian of Hawai'i, has made a distinction between new *malihini* haoles who arrived in the early twentieth century and the old *kama'āina* haole elite that had come to the islands shortly after Captain Cook's arrival and firmly established themselves by the end of the nineteenth century. Theon Wright, a longtime resident of Honolulu, uses these terms in *Rape in Paradise,* showing his famil-iarity with local terminology.[20] Diversity existed within the haole community as a whole, but in general there was a great gap between the white community and that of nonwhites. To use Fuchs' words, though *malihini* haoles like the Massies were not necessarily "born to rule" in the same ways that *kama'āina* haoles were, "most of them quickly took their places in the ethnic-social class system of the Islands, a position distinctly above the other ethnic groups with respect to educational and occupational opportunity."[21]

The long history of planter and merchant power in Hawai'i was what linked both white groups, old and new. The increasing numbers of U.S. mil-itary, the prevalence of an English-language press, and the persistence of an American educational system—all of these factors in the early decades of the twentieth century further cemented the dominance of whites in the Territory of Hawai'i.

American dominance included powerful ideologies from the continent that were then transplanted onto the terrain of Hawai'i. A language of white domination, brought by planters in the nineteenth century, meshed well with the sentiments of southern military personnel who came to Hawai'i during the 1920s and 1930s. Decades of missionary and planter hegemony had firmly established "white ways" in the islands that furthered colonial domination of indigenous Native Hawaiians and of the large numbers of immigrants of color brought in to serve as laborers on sugar plantations. Although the ideology of white domination was not expressed by every haole, the belief in white superiority linked many haoles, old and newly arrived, in their support of Thalia Massie and in defense of "white womanhood."

It was within this ideology that poor whites and elite territorial and military officials found common ground. Though from vastly different socioeconomic backgrounds, poor white sailors, for example, could align themselves with white elites in the defense of white womanhood during the Massie case. Edward Lord and Albert Jones were two such enlisted men hired by the Massie family to protect Thalia and later to force a confession out of Joseph Kahahawai. The class position of these military men was validated both by their white skin and by their involvement in the military as a dominating force in the islands. Even though men like Lord and Jones earned scarcely more than working-class locals, they were compensated by what W. E. B. Du Bois called a "public and psychological wage."[22] They believed in their superiority as white men.

The United States established itself as a military presence in Hawai'i in the late nineteenth century, after its negotiation of Pearl Harbor as a port. But by the 1930s the economic and social effects of its presence and continued growth put a strain on Hawai'i's political economy. In Honolulu the city's population grew by 250 percent in the first three decades, from 39,306 in 1900 to 137,582 in 1930. In the estimation of Andrew Lind, this population growth was "more rapid than the expansion of occupational opportunity, and the intensive competition within the city constitutes a threat to the stability of race relations in the Islands." Lind calculated that the military as an industry added approximately "27,000 wage-earners and perhaps 10,000 women and children as additional consumers to the population by 1936." In 1933 about three thousand of these new employees were civilians from the local population, and military spending in the territory was $13.8 million for that year.[23]

The Depression years brought added stress to the city's inhabitants. In economic hard times, racial tensions in Honolulu worsened. Formal and informal policies of segregation separated whites from a nonwhite, local population. Even those whites who did not favor segregation experienced a life in Hawai'i that was quite different from that enjoyed by locals.

THE GEOGRAPHY OF WHITE HONOLULU

Local consciousness and identity were formed along lines of geographic opposition. During the Massie case, Thalia Massie's story of rape revealed a clear boundary that had emerged and evolved within the geography of Honolulu. Mānoa Valley was one area that some whites hoped would remain a protected place of privilege. The creation and maintenance of this *physical* social space depended on the ideology of an *imagined* social space: Mānoa was a geographic site where haoles were attempting to replicate racial hierarchies established on the continent that separated white from nonwhite.

By the third decade of the twentieth century Mānoa was already the domain of a substantial haole population, but it was not the only self-segregated area for whites on the island of Oʻahu: the censuses of 1920 and 1930 showed that haoles lived in the Honolulu districts of ʻAlewa Heights, Pacific Heights, Makiki Heights, upper Nuʻuanu Valley, Waikīkī, and Maunalani.[24] In the same year that Thalia and Thomas Massie moved to Mānoa, John Wesley Coulter and Alfred Gomes Serrao of the University of Hawaiʻi conducted fieldwork in the valley to study its economic and social geography. In the spring of 1930 Coulter and Serrao counted approximately one thousand homes in the valley. A remarkable 80 percent—eight hundred homes—were inhabited by "Caucasians of North European origin." Japanese comprised the next largest group, making up 17 percent of the residents in Mānoa. The remaining 3 percent consisted of Chinese, Portuguese, Native Hawaiian, Puerto Rican, Filipino, and Spanish.[25]

Mānoa was not exclusively white by the early 1930s, but it was home to increasing numbers of military officers' families. The valley was also home to the University of Hawaiʻi (founded as a land-grant college in 1907), small farms, a poi factory, and a few locals. Beginning in the late 1920s one section of the valley was rented out by military officers and their families who preferred to live off base. Mānoa was one of the few areas on Oʻahu where concentrations of military families lived. The experiences of these newly arrived whites were linked to older white communities through participation in social activities—activities quite separate from those of nonwhite locals.

Life for haoles in places like Mānoa Valley was a world apart from that of locals. It seemed especially easy for military wives. Grace Fortescue wrote a letter to her mother describing the life of leisure she enjoyed in her moments away from the Ala Moana assault trial. By her own account, she had time for lawn bowling and learning the hula. Fortescue also provided her perspective on living in Honolulu as a white woman. Aware of the racial tensions in the city, she couched her view of social relations in terms of a general fear of nonwhite crime committed against whites: "Honolulu is sitting on a volcano literally and figuratively. The volcano is in [*sic*] another island and we haven't been over to see it erupt, but the volcanic tension here is due to the crime wave [and] is enormous. Two criminals escaped from jail last week. One entered a white woman's house and raped her and tied her up—He has been caught but the other one is still at large and consequently everyone carries a gun and shoots at the slightest provocation." In this passage Fortescue showed her awareness of the physical and social environment around her; she used the volcano on the Big Island as a metaphoric means to express the explosive nature of race relations in Honolulu. She continued her narrative of danger, telling her mother that white women were carrying guns to defend themselves especially when their husbands were away: "I wish you could see us coming home from the movies after dark. I drove the car, Hélène in the middle with her .22 and Thalia on the outside[,] her Army automatic cocked and pointing out the window. We looked like an arsenal on wheels. Tommie was on duty so we were alone."[26]

WHITE ANXIETIES: FEAR OF CRIME

Especially during the Depression, most people living in Honolulu would have agreed that general racial tensions existed between whites and nonwhites. The haole population, however, was less likely to see these tensions as the result of a lack of job and educational opportunities, combined with the existence of substandard wages and work conditions. These realities were far more likely to be noticed by working-class locals. The haole population, on the other hand, tended to see racial tension as a possible threat to white persons and white property. The *Honolulu Advertiser* and the *Honolulu Times* accommodated wealthy owners by stirring up a generalized fear of a crime wave. Selected politicians, editors at the major newspapers, and navy officials racialized working-class locals like the Kaluwela Boys, painting them as criminals, organized community groups to deal with the perceived rise in crime, and blamed locals for their own poverty. Instead of seeing whiteness as privilege, haoles in Honolulu viewed themselves as possible victims, not acknowledging that whites were more often oppressors than oppressed.[27]

A few years before the Massie case white residents in particular were concerned with what they saw as an increase in crime, including rape, in Honolulu. Sociologist Peter Nelligan has shown that police statistics and detailed descriptions of crimes against whites as reported in the *Honolulu Advertiser* were successful in prompting modest changes in law enforcement in the late 1920s. Major change, however, would not come until after the Massie case.[28] Women's groups were instrumental in generating support for these changes. The League of Women Voters and the Citizens' Organization for Good Government were two of the largest organizations to criticize Governor Judd and called upon him to restructure law enforcement in Honolulu. The league played a smaller role in voicing its opinions on the Massie case; it was largely concerned with calls to place women on juries and to get women involved more directly in the police force. The league often did not directly comment on the conduct of the trials of the Massie case. The Citizens' Organization, however, was created in direct response to the Massie trials. Its members were usually also members of the League of Women Voters, and its leaders were the wives of prominent men in the islands. Mrs. Anne Kluegel, for example, was the wife of Henry Kluegel, supervisor of the Kalaupapa colony for Hansen's disease patients on the island of Moloka'i.[29] Mrs. Louise Dillingham was the wife of Walter Dillingham, a man whose business success in dredging and construction rivaled the power of Big Five industry elites. In short, white women in Hawai'i were a force to be reckoned with.

WHITE DISCOURSE:
THE STRUCTURE AND LANGUAGE
OF THE HAOLE POPULATION

> Socially the whites form a village within the city, and this small village has the limitations and the advantages of its size; almost everyone knows everything about everybody. The newspapers publish the news, while the word-of-mouth carries the gossip, scandal, conjecture and rumor which makes three-fourths of the conversation of the Islanders.
>
> —*From "White Honolulu" chapter of Don Blanding's* Hula Moons
> (NEW YORK: DODD, MEAD, AND COMPANY, 1930)

For many white residents and visitors, Honolulu of the 1930s exhibited many features of a small town for white social elites. The lives of military officers and their touring families and friends, and the activities of planters and merchants were almost common knowledge. The weekly *Honolulu Times* and the daily *Honolulu Advertiser* frequently announced the comings and goings of these prominent residents and visitors to the islands. Tourists visited Hawai'i to take part in—and perpetuate the myth of—the paradise that they had become familiar with through reading or from the comments of previous visitors. During the Massie case features artist and columnist Fay King found it difficult to imagine Honolulu as anything other than "serenely beautiful like its sad, sweet melodies."[30] Even during the height of the case Thalia Massie's mother was eager to report to relatives on the East Coast that despite the emotional difficulties Thalia faced during the trial, Honolulu was a wonderful place where she could enjoy a variety of activities with her younger daughter, sixteen-year-old Hélène Fortescue.

Through print media, whites in Hawai'i and on the continent could imagine and produce a separate Honolulu of privilege for themselves. The city and other sections of the islands were areas to be enjoyed. In early twentieth-century Honolulu most whites were either temporary residents—tourists or military personnel—or members of the planter and merchant class that ruled the islands. By contrast, people of color were either Native Hawaiian inhabitants or the descendants of immigrants who had come to the islands to work.

ACTIVITIES AND MOVEMENT:
WHITE ELITES AND RECREATION

The activities of navy wives highlight the vast differences in the lives of locals and nonlocals. Women like Thalia Massie had more leisure time than working-class local women, for example. Massie had time for afternoon tea parties, enrolling part-time in classes at the University of Hawai'i, and accompanying officers and their wives to clubs in Waikīkī.

Military families like the Massies did not always set down roots in the same way that locals did. Members of these families were often visitors, staying for a year or two en route to another military post. They often did not have time to accustom themselves to the variety of racial and ethnic groups in the islands. More often than not, their cultural frames of reference were the regions of the United States in which they grew up. Many military personnel and other new haole arrivals to Hawaiʻi during the 1920s and 1930s came from the American South and West Coast.[31] The Massies were not unusual in this regard: Thalia was the descendant of a southern family that had moved to the District of Columbia, and Thomasʼ family hailed from the state of Kentucky.

Military visitors and tourists affirmed their identity not by linking themselves to Hawaiʻi as a place, but by conducting themselves as they would on the continent. They toured parts of the islands knowing that they did not have to live there.[32] Their social activities replicated the privileges of whiteness that they enjoyed on the continent. In the case of Grace Fortescue and her two daughters, leisure activities brought them into contact with other whites from other exclusive neighborhoods. Since Thomas Massie was an officer, he and his family did not have to stay on base or limit their social activities to Pearl Harbor. Lieutenant Massie chose to live in Mānoa, and when his mother-in-law came to join them, she also rented a bungalow in the valley on Kolowalu Street.[33]

On September 12, 1931, the Massies and their navy set traveled to Waikīkī for a night of enjoyment and stepped into a zone with potential for danger.[34] Waikīkī was the playground for a variety of social groups; it was home to some local people, but the section near the *ewa* end of the Ala Wai canal was a recreational zone where races and classes mingled and sometimes came into conflict with one another.

A DEFENSE OF WHITE
WOMANHOOD: THE EVENTS
OF THE MASSIE CASE

Saturday Night, September 12, 1931: Navy Night in Waikīkī

Saturday nights at the Ala Wai Inn were called "Navy Night"; many locals thus stayed away, preferring not to mingle with the officers and their wives.[35] Those who did visit the inn that night were neatly dressed, but the local men certainly did not wear coats like Thomas Massie, nor did the local women wear formal dresses like Thalia Massieʼs green one that evening.[36] Thalia had not really wanted to go out that night and had argued with her husband over dinner about it. In fact, their marriage seemed to have been a hasty and unhappy one, with Thalia having married "Tommie" in September 1927, when she was only sixteen. (She apparently married, in part, to escape her overbearing mother and dispassionate father.)[37] But on that Saturday in September Thomas had promised fellow officers at Pearl Harbor that he and Thalia would join them and their wives at an informal gathering at the Ala Wai Inn later in the evening.

The Massies found the inn to be quite crowded when they arrived, but they were able to secure a small dining alcove.[38] Though Prohibition was in effect, patrons brought *ōkolehao,* a bootleg drink, and had it at their tables. Joseph Freitas, the half-Hawaiian, half-Portuguese doorkeeper, looked out for any federal agents so he could quickly tell customers to hide their drinks from view. He was a keen observer who also noticed that Thalia (whom he knew then only as a white woman in a green dress) had arrived with the Jerry Branson party, her head down as if she were brooding or possibly even drunk.[39] Thalia, according to many in attendance, did not want to be there and managed to argue with Thomas' friend, Ralph Stogsdall, who then swore at her. Thalia slapped Stogsdall and then walked away from him and the rest of her husband's friends.[40] Sometime around 11:30 p.m. Thalia left the inn alone and wandered down John 'Ena Road.

Thomas looked for Thalia at the inn but decided to stay and not worry too much about the whereabouts of his wife. Later he drove with Jerry Branson to the house of James "Red" Rigby, one of Thomas' shipmates, and used the phone to call home. It was 1:30 a.m., according to the Japanese maid who lived and worked at the Rigby house.[41] Thalia told her husband, "Come home at once. *Something terrible has happened.*"[42]

When Thomas arrived home he called the Honolulu police at around 1:45 a.m. to report that his wife had been assaulted by a group of Hawaiian men.[43] The fact that it was Thomas, not Thalia, who called the police prompted some locals to speculate later that perhaps he or some other naval officer had beaten Thalia and then fabricated a story about a "gang of Hawaiians" for the police. Questions remained, however: where had Thalia been? What happened to her between 11:30 p.m. Saturday night and 1:30 a.m. Sunday morning? According to the testimony she gave to Inspector John McIntosh within hours of her attack, a car had approached her from behind on John 'Ena Road and stopped. Two men she believed to be Hawaiians dragged her into the car, and one put his hand over her mouth. The two held her down in the back seat while she begged them to let her go. The driver drove to the quarantine station on Ala Moana Road, where Thalia said she was pulled out of the car and into the bushes. There she said she was "assaulted six or seven times."[44]

Afterward, Thalia wandered down Ala Moana Road in search of help and waved down a passing automobile occupied by Mr. and Mrs. Eustace Bellinger. When they stopped, Thalia's first words betrayed how she equated safety with race: before accepting assistance, she asked the Bellingers, "Are you white people?"[45]

The Ala Moana Assault Trial

The Ala Moana assault trial itself, formally known as *The Territory of Hawaii v. Ben Ahakuelo, et al.,* started on November 18 and went to the jury on December 3, 1931.[46] As soon as jury selection began on November 16 and 17, navy and territorial officials were concerned about the racial and ethnic makeup of the jury. Of the twelve men selected, seven were white (including one Portuguese) and five were nonwhite. Two of the five nonwhites were Chinese American, two were Japanese American, and one was Native Hawaiian.[47]

> John G. Botello, Portuguese (sometimes considered "white," or "local"), Honolulu Iron Works employee
> William Brede, white, Honolulu Iron Works employee
> Ernest H. Fountain, white, Aloha Motors employee
> Robert French, white, Schumann Carriage Company employee
> Takeo Kuamoto, Japanese, American Factors (a Big Five firm) employee
> Jan Yip Lee, Chinese, Hawaii Shoe Company employee
> Matsuo Matsugama, Japanese, Theo. T. Davies, Ltd. (a Big Five firm) employee
> William E. Paikuli, Native Hawaiian, employed by the city engineer
> Hee Wai, Chinese, City & County of Honolulu employee
> John Watson, white, Mutual Telephone Company employee

Seated in the jury box, these men of color were in stark contrast to the court observers, who were mostly white women, with some Native Hawaiian and Portuguese women at the back of the courtroom.[48] The territorial prosecutors in the case were two white men, Griffith Wight and Eddie Sylva; in contrast, the lawyers defending the various Kauluwela Boys were men of color, except one. William Heen, a part-Hawaiian lawyer and former Circuit Court judge, represented Ben Ahakuelo and Henry Chang. Robert Murakami, one of the first Japanese Americans to be admitted to the bar in the territory, was assisted by Chinese American Ernest Kai in representing David Takai. William Pittman, the sole white attorney for the defendants and a longtime resident of Hawai'i, represented Joe Kahahawai and Horace Ida.[49]

In court Thalia said she left the Ala Wai Inn "shortly after 11:30" because she was "bored and tired of the party."[50] While on the stand she pointed to Kahahawai and Chang, indicating that they had dragged her into a car on the night of September 12. She identified the third man in the car as Ben Ahakuelo and said she recognized him in the courtroom by his gold tooth. Two months before the trial, when asked about her assailants on the night of her attack, Thalia had told Inspector McIntosh that they were Hawaiians. In the early morning hours of September 13, when she first gave her statement to police, she admitted that she had not seen the faces of her attackers and could identify them "only by their voices."[51] She identified Horace Ida by the leather coat he was wearing but could not really recall David Takai.[52] Jury members and those following the trial transcripts in the local papers noticed the discrepancies in her stories. There seemed to be a marked difference in the amount of detail that she had given to Honolulu detectives on September 13 when compared to what she provided during the trial. While some reasoned that trauma might have caused her reticence in the hours immediately after the attack, her attention to detail during the November trial was considered quite exceptional.

WHITE SENTIMENTS:
RESPONSES TO THE ALA MOANA
ASSAULT TRIAL

In the eyes of the haole community and even the local population, the Ala Moana assault trial revealed the inadequacies of the Honolulu Police Department in collecting evidence. While both communities called for police reform, elements of the haole community were certainly more vocal. The League of Women Voters of Hawaii held a special meeting on December 30, 1931, to discuss what it perceived to be a rise in sex crimes in Honolulu. Earlier in December the league had expressed dissatisfaction with the Honolulu Police Department and held a rummage sale in order to fund a special task force on sex crimes. One of its own recommendations was that women be admitted to the police force to serve as matrons, instructing youths of the community to stay away from criminal activity. The league's meeting minutes also featured a regular report on a rape bill being considered by the territorial legislature.[53]

Mrs. Kluegel started her Citizens' Organization for Good Government on January 4, just four days before Joseph Kahahawai was killed, and met at the Young Hotel on a weekly basis. The group seems to have been organized not only as a result of Thalia Massie's alleged rape on September 12–13, 1931, but also because of the recent alleged rape of Mrs. James Odowda on January 2, 1932.[54]

White women in Hawai'i also called for active change in the territory's legal system. In late January 1932 Territorial Delegate to Congress Victor Houston responded to his female constituency by pushing a bill in Washington, D.C., that would allow women of the territory to be selected for jury duty. The League of Women Voters of Hawaii had been pushing for women on juries as early as 1929; the mistrial of the Ala Moana assault trial was a strong influence in urging politicians like Houston to respond once again.[55] Governor Judd also responded to the calls of women to hold a special session of the territorial legislature to consider a number of acts. The first act would reorganize the police department.[56] The tenth act would be a victory for groups like the league because it set the punishment for rape in the territory as "death" or "hard labor for life or any number of years, in the discretion of the court." The act also strengthened rape law in the Territory of Hawai'i by qualifying a rape victim as a "competent witness" in her alleged rape, abduction, or seduction. Governor Judd signed this act into law and it took effect on January 29, 1932.[57] Before the law, claimants of rape like Thalia Massie had to have their allegations "corroborated by evidence other than her own" and had to "prove beyond a reasonable doubt, each material element of the crime."[58]

When the Ala Moana assault trial ended in a mistrial on December 6, 1931, many members of the haole community felt that justice had not been served. Though a second trial was scheduled for the near future, a small group chose to take the law into their own hands sooner. On December 12, 1931, several navy men abducted Horace Ida from a downtown speakeasy, took him to the Pali lookout, a famous historical cliff on O'ahu, and threatened to throw him over if he did not confess to the rape of Thalia Massie. Though badly bruised, he managed to escape with his life. On January 8, 1932, Thomas Massie, Grace Fortescue, Edward Lord, and Albert Jones kidnapped Joseph Kahahawai from the front of the judiciary building, Ali'iōlani

Hale, and attempted to coerce a confession out of him at gunpoint. What happened to Kahahawai at the Massies' rented bungalow in Mānoa is not clear except for the fact that he was shot through the heart and died almost immediately.[59]

Shortly after a *Honolulu Advertiser* reporter confronted Thalia Massie with news of Kahahawai's kidnapping and murder, she responded, "I am sorry this man has been shot, but it was no more than he deserved." She saw the death of Kahahawai as just. She also continued a narrative of a need for safety and the defense of white women in Honolulu. She told the *Advertiser* reporter, "I have been protected at all times by the shore patrol and have carried my revolver constantly as I do not think this town is safe for any woman." She also linked her story to that of Mrs. Odowda, the white woman whom escaped convict Lui Kaikapu, a Native Hawaiian, had allegedly raped less than a week earlier, on January 2: "I am very sorry for this poor girl at Wilhelmina Rise for I know just what she went through." She framed her story around a general call for law and order: "I am glad Kaikapu was caught and put in jail and hope the rest of those who assaulted me will be put into jail as soon as possible."[60]

Both the beating of Horace Ida and the killing of Joseph Kahahawai were carried out by a minority of the haole community in Honolulu. Public sentiment indicated, however, that large numbers of whites in Hawaiʻi and on the continent condoned these extralegal measures. Newspaper editorials, the remarks of navy brass, and letters to territorial officials confirmed this sentiment and sent a clear message: a boundary existed between white women and men of color, and any transgression of that border was to be enforced through vigilantism if necessary.[61]

Honolulu was not the American South, but the recent arrival of southerners to the islands via military service ensured that its racial hierarchies would apply in Hawaiʻi as well.[62] Thalia Massie's story of rape was told in the context of a pattern of white dominance imported from the continent, a history of a haole oligarchy in the islands since the late nineteenth century, and a general but unwritten rule affirming the status of whites over nonwhites throughout the United States. Locals in Hawaiʻi defined themselves against this hegemonic sense of white privilege.

3

THE KILLING OF JOSEPH KAHAHAWAI

Native Hawaiians and
Stories of Resistance

Poor Kahahawai! These haoles murdered you in cold blood. They
did the same thing to my brother. They shoot and kill us Hawaiians.
We do not shoot haoles, but they shoot us! Never mind — the truth
will come out! Poor boy, God will keep you. We will do the rest. . . .

—*David Kama's eulogy for Joseph Kahahawai, Puea Cemetery,
Kalihi-Pālama,* JANUARY 10, 1932[1]

THE FUNERAL OF Joseph Kahahawai was a mass gathering for Native Hawaiians
and non–Native Hawaiians alike. Friends, relatives, and those sympathetic to
Kahahawai's family as victims of injustice attended the funeral. By one estimation over two thousand people attended. David Kama publicly mourned
the loss of Joe. Kama's brother had been killed years before in an altercation
with a haole soldier, so his words understandably resonated with many in the
audience.

This chapter examines how Native Hawaiian struggles in the early decades of the twentieth century often allowed Hawaiians to align themselves
on the side of working-class Asians, Portuguese, Puerto Ricans, and other locals.[2] The death of Kahahawai in January 1932 at the hands of four mainland

haoles served to solidify the interests of Native Hawaiians as similar to those of other working-class people of color. These interests challenged the tenuous and contradictory alliances that Native Hawaiian elites had sometimes formed with white merchants, planters, and governing officials who sought desperately to preserve their oligarchic control of territorial Hawai'i.

During the first three decades of life under an American political system, the cultural terrain of Hawai'i changed dramatically. Native Hawaiians merged traditional cultural practices with the political forms of the dominant culture, ultimately presenting themselves as a powerful force in the territory. Native Hawaiian elites had formed political alliances with haole elites over the years, but by the time of the Massie case the killing of Joseph Kahahawai came to be seen as more than merely an injury against the Native Hawaiian community. Kahahawai's murder was cast as a story of local oppression, revealing to Native Hawaiians that they had more in common with working-class peoples of color and were part of an emerging local culture.

A HISTORY OF AGENCY
AMID INJUSTICE

Native Hawaiians suffered injustices, often at the hands of haole and other populations that had settled in the islands since Captain Cook's arrival in 1778. Focusing solely on the victimization of Native Hawaiians, however, obscures the history of Native Hawaiian agency and modes of resistance in the nineteenth and twentieth centuries. Native Hawaiian men and women made their own history, even if it was not always under conditions of their choosing.

Not all Native Hawaiians were working class, but during the Massie case Native Hawaiians often transcended the boundaries of class in order to articulate a critique of a legal system and racial hierarchy that had allowed for the lynching of Joseph Kahahawai, one of their own. What linked these Native Hawaiians was not necessarily identity politics based on racial or ethnic affiliation alone. This chapter examines how macrolevel electoral politics was also influenced by the day-to-day cultural politics of communal activities and practices that served to define local group interests as different from those of a white elite.[3] Instead, knowledge of injustices suffered for more than one hundred years since the first encounter with the West gave Native Hawaiians—rich and poor—a sense of common ground. The Massie case was yet another narrative told among the Native Hawaiian community about the need to respond to violence and injustice at the hands of whites.

Native Hawaiians had reason to be upset. The nineteenth century had taken its toll on their population, which may have been as high as 800,000 at the time of Captain Cook's arrival in 1778.[4] Later, in 1820, American Congregationalist missionaries had come from Boston and introduced Christianity and literacy to the islands. By the middle of the nineteenth century the Hawaiian language had a standardized orthography, and large numbers of Native Hawaiians were educated in writing both English and Hawaiian. Men like David Malo and, later, Samuel Kamakau were able to record the history, or *mo'olelo*, of Hawai'i and publish their accounts in serial form in Hawaiian- and English-language newspapers.

The mid-nineteenth century, however, also witnessed the drastic reorganization of land tenure, the 1848 Mahele. Sometimes known as the Great Mahele, this division of land further dispossessed Native Hawaiians in general and was especially damaging to the large number of common Native Hawaiians, or *maka 'āinana*. Shortly after 1848 provisions were made so that *maka 'āinana* could petition for plots of their own land. Few took advantage of this opportunity since they were unfamiliar with Western land law, or were completely unaware that the Mahele had taken place. The majority of the *maka 'āinana* during mid-century lived in rural areas or on neighbor islands, distant from Honolulu, where the land claims had to be registered.

Throughout the nineteenth century the *ali'i*, or chiefly class, guaranteed for themselves a measure of autonomy. Shortly after Captain Cook's arrival at the end of the eighteenth century *ali'i* like Kamehameha the Great quickly realized that uniting as a nation would secure for Native Hawaiians a chance to be recognized as a nation-state on par with other nations. By the early nineteenth century Kamehameha had united all the islands except Kaua'i, whose chief would eventually defer to Kamehameha in 1810. With the exception of brief interruptions in the 1840s, Native Hawaiians had a sovereign nation for nearly a century.

By the 1890s Native Hawaiians had declined in number and had lost much of their land, as well as their political representation. Queen Lili'uokalani was overthrown in 1893, and then there was a period of rule under the provisional government, followed by the Republic of Hawaii, both headed by American businessmen. In 1898 the United States annexed Hawai'i solely through a joint resolution of Congress rather than an internationally recognized treaty.[5] With the Organic Act in 1900, Hawai'i became officially known as the Territory of Hawai'i.[6] Increasing involvement with the United States disempowered centuries-old *ali'i* and the more recent Native Hawaiian monarchy. But in some cases the prestige of royal status lent well to social prestige; during the Massie case Abigail Kawananakoa (1882–1945), wife of Prince David Kawananakoa (1868–1908), who had been in the line of succession to the throne, figured prominently in defending the rights of working-class Native Hawaiians, formerly known as the *maka 'āinana*.[7]

For the most part, the *maka 'āinana* suffered greatly in the century after contact with the West. By the early decades of the twentieth century their descendants were often members of the working class. Annexation had made the connection to the political economy of the United States more permanent, and hence more painful, for working-class Native Hawaiians. The Depression hit worldwide, but it hit working-class areas like Kalihi-Pālama especially hard.

Annexation, however, had some curious benefits, which Native Hawaiians and other locals would use to their advantage, especially during times of crisis, like the Massie case. With annexation and the provisions of the Organic Act, a majority of the territory's residents automatically became U.S. citizens. In the early twentieth century these citizens were largely whites, Native Hawaiians, and second-generation Chinese and Japanese who had been born in Hawai'i. By 1930 more than 130,000 of the territory's 368,000 residents were citizens over the age of twenty-one; the census also showed that 91,082 of these citizens were males over twenty-one and eligible to vote for their territorial officials and delegates to Congress. Though disease, poor living conditions, and dispossession of their land had severely decreased their numbers, Native Hawaiians and part–Native Hawaiians made up a large part of the electorate: more than 10,000 were eligible voters. The haole elite that ruled the Territory of Hawai'i had more than 22,000 eligible voters and sought to form an alliance with Native Hawaiians in order to counter what they called the "Oriental vote."[8]

The haole elite had always realized the need to broker its ability to rule with Native Hawaiian elites, even before annexation made the power of the electorate extremely important in a government that obeyed federal laws. By the time Joseph Kahahawai was killed in 1932, Native Hawaiians were very powerful in the electorate. Though the Massie-Fortescue group and the navy did not seem overly concerned about Native Hawaiian opinion during the

early months of 1932, Big Five business leaders, territorial officials, and other members of the haole elite in Hawai'i knew that the killing of a Native
Hawaiian by whites created a delicate situation indeed. Whereas the Massie
case largely represented a concern about rape and the safety of white women,
after the kidnapping and murder of Kahahawai, the case centered on issues of
injustice against Native Hawaiians (with Kahahawai serving as a martyr for
the local population) and the inability of territorial government to stand up
to federal powers.

The killing of Kahahawai also made the case even more of a spectacle. For
continental Americans, the new twist made for greater intrigue—how often,
after all, is a group of East Coast socialites caught red-handed for murder?
For those in Hawai'i Kahahawai's murder was an injustice not only against
Native Hawaiians, but against the local population as a whole.

THE FUNERAL OF
JOSEPH KAHAHAWAI

Native Hawaiians had spoken out about the Massie case earlier, but the killing
of Kahahawai spurred them to speak out even more. Kahahawai's funeral on
January 10, 1932, was a focal point for the multiple meanings of the Massie
case. David Kama gave voice to an opinion that many others shared, and his
words are some of the few made by working-class Native Hawaiians that were
recorded that day. Most newspaper reports mentioned that the circumstances
of Kahahawai's death and the proceedings of the Massie case were no doubt
discussed by the thousands in attendance, but only in whispers. The funeral
was great cause for concern among territorial officials, the Honolulu police,
and the U.S. Navy because all knew the potential for violence.

Of all the newspapers in the territory, the *Star-Bulletin* carried the most
detailed coverage of the funeral. Like the *Honolulu Advertiser* and the *Nippu
Jiji* (a leading Japanese- and English-language newspaper), the *Star-Bulletin*
characterized the Kahahawai funeral as the largest held for any Native Hawaiian not of royalty, with over two thousand people in attendance at the
Puea Cemetery in Kalihi-Pālama, located on School Street near Houghtailing
Street.[9] The *Advertiser* gave a more conservative estimate of fifteen hundred
people in the crowd, while the *Nippu Jiji* estimated twenty-five hundred. The
more "local" or "ethnic" the newspaper, the larger the estimated attendance
for the funeral.

Native Hawaiians made up the vast majority of the crowd, but there were representatives from all sectors of the community. As the *Star-Bulletin* remarked, "Most of those present were Hawaiians, but there was to be seen in the crowd an occasional 'haole' face as well as the faces of a number of Japanese, Chinese, Portuguese, and other races."[10] In this respect, those present were largely representative of the working-class community of locals of which Kahahawai had been a part during his lifetime. Two area football clubs, the Hui Eleu Athletic Club and the Kakaako Sons, sent floral wreaths as expressions of their sympathy. Territorial representative Harry T. Mills of the Kalihi District was in attendance, as were two prominent Native Hawaiians, Senator Ernest A. K. Akina of the Kohala District on the Big Island and Jonah Kumalae, editor of the Hawaiian- and English-language newspaper *Ke Alakai O Hawaii*.[11]

Kahahawai's body was on view at the Nuuanu Funeral Parlor from Saturday evening until it was transported Sunday morning to the downtown Fort Street Cathedral of Our Lady of Peace for a Catholic funeral service. Ben Ahakuelo, Henry Chang, Horace Ida, and David Takai viewed the body earlier that Sunday morning at the funeral parlor, paying their last respects there; they were not present at the Catholic service or the burial site for fear of a possible riot. Later, the Honolulu police returned these four young men to the city jail, where they had requested to stay for their own safety after the abduction and killing of their friend the previous Friday night.

THE FEAR OF A RIOT

Territorial officials, the police, and the navy all feared a possible riot at Kahahawai's funeral. Uniformed police were stationed at the funeral parlor all Saturday night, and six officers accompanied the Kauluwela Boys when they viewed Kahahawai's body. Police motorcycles escorted the large procession from the downtown cathedral to the cemetery, where plainclothes officers mingled with the crowd as a precaution. More than one hundred police were on patrol that day, with fifty held in reserve at the National Guard in case of emergency. Surprisingly, the *Star-Bulletin* (but not the conservative and safety-minded *Advertiser*) informed the general public of these added police measures. At the time, law enforcement in the territory was in the beginning stages of a thorough revision: High Sheriff John C. Lane left his office at the request of Governor Judd after Kahahawai was killed. The *Star-Bulletin* also reported that the navy wisely postponed shore leave for its personnel during the weekend of the Kahahawai funeral.[12]

Officials knew that a coordinated Native Hawaiian revolt was unlikely, but they feared that a series of disturbances would occur between the increasing numbers of military personnel and the locals in Honolulu's congested urban areas. Throughout the duration of the case naval shore leave was often postponed or held in areas like Hilo on the Big Island.[13] Less than a month earlier, in December, naval officials, territorial officials, and police had feared riots between locals and military personnel following the kidnapping of Horace Ida on the 13th, in broad daylight, by a band of U.S. Navy sailors who subsequently drove him into Nuʻuanu Valley, beat him, and threatened to throw him over the Pali if he did not confess to the rape of Thalia Massie.

Weekends were especially worrisome for officials since that was when locals and military personnel often traveled to Waikīkī and other areas of Honolulu known for their common and popular recreation spots. During the weekend after Ida's beating there were "a few sporadic brawls," but no widespread rioting. On Saturday, December 20, the City and County of Honolulu put a double shift of police officers on duty; these forces were augmented by the navy shore patrol and army military police.[14]

The earlier beating of Ida had provoked the ire of both Japanese American and Native Hawaiian groups. What upset both groups the most was the cavalier and dismissive attitude that navy officials displayed toward the local population and the local economy. On the weekend of Ida's beating, Rear Admiral George Pettengill, commander of minecraft forces in Hawaiʻi at the time, assured readers of the *Star-Bulletin* in an interview that it was his job to keep his personnel "out of this mess." He assured readers that he would have no sympathy for sailors if they were found to have been involved. Pettengill believed, however, that it was up to civil authorities to bring Ida's assailants to justice.[15] The *Nippu Jiji* reported that Native Hawaiians in the Hawaiian Civic Club objected to Admiral Pettengill's public declaration that Honolulu was presently unsafe for women.[16]

Native Hawaiians, Japanese Americans, and other locals in Hawaiʻi were cognizant of the power of the press. Locals voiced their discontent, thus spurring naval officials to clarify their statements after earlier remarks had fueled hysteria. Even the most casual of remarks could damage area business. For example, in one instance Rear Admiral Stirling clarified the Honolulu situation for continental Americans: "Sensational reports said to have been published in mainland papers are unwarranted. There has been no rioting. The authorities are watching the situation and have it under control."[17] In this case the navy responded to local pressure, but also asserted that it was in control of "the situation." Throughout the case navy officials skillfully created rumors that served their interests and squelched others that did not.[18] Thus on a daily basis politics was involved in whatever appeared in newspapers. Over time these micropolitical events accumulated and had a larger effect on electoral politics: if a paper could characterize a certain administration or political party as more adept at keeping the city under control, perhaps voters would be inclined to support these politicians and their respective parties in future elections. Both locals and nonlocals acknowledged the press' unique ability to shape public opinion—and nothing could stir the public more than an expressed concern for its safety.[19]

RANGE OF RESPONSES

Joseph Kahahawai's funeral was yet another occasion used by the navy to infuriate locals. Native Hawaiians in particular were upset when Admiral William Pratt made a callous remark shortly after Kahahawai's murder suggesting that lynch law should prevail when the territory's court system failed.[20] On the morning of the funeral, Reverend H. H. Leavitt, pastor of the Central Union Church, was one of many religious leaders to voice an objection to lynch law. Rear Admiral Stirling's sentiments were similar to those of Admiral Pratt, and when he published his memoirs in 1939, Stirling came close to endorsing lynch law and made other disparaging remarks about Native Hawaiians. Commenting on Kahahawai's kidnapping and murder, he said, "I had half expected, in spite of discipline, to hear that one or more [of the Kauluwela Boys] had been found swinging from trees by the neck up Nuuana [*sic*] Valley or at the Pali."[21]

Native Hawaiians rebuked lynch law, just as other locals and continental American groups began doing in early 1932. Hawaiian objections, however, revealed the viewpoint of a native people that had been victimized for over a century. Unlike editors from *The Nation* and other liberal presses, as well as groups that pressed the need to support a strong court system, Native Hawaiians focused more on the personal and communal injury sustained by the Kahahawai family and the Native Hawaiian community. Joseph Kahahawai Sr. reiterated his son's innocence in a short address at the mortuary: "I talked frequently with my son following his arrest. I asked him to tell me if he was innocent or guilty of the crime for which he was held and he said that he was innocent. I asked him about the case repeatedly and he repeatedly told me that he was not guilty of wrongdoing." He continued, emphasizing his son's character and belief in God, "During the lifetime of my boy, I have never known him to do anything objectionable. He was always a good boy who was well liked by everyone who knew him. I asked Joseph to take an oath before god and he said, 'Daddy, I swear before God that I never did anything wrong.'"[22]

By examining Kahahawai's funeral in detail, we can see in general how some Native Hawaiians merged traditional cultural practices with dominant forms of Western and American culture. In particular, the actions of those attending the funeral show how Native Hawaiian language and attitudes were often combined with Christian beliefs and idioms. The Kahahawai family, as Catholic, was perhaps part of a slight minority of the population, but they were Christian, like many other Native Hawaiians by the early twentieth century. Joseph Kahahawai had also attended St. Louis School, a Catholic high school and college that was one of the first private schools in the territory to accept nonwhites as part of its student body.

From time to time the Kahahawai family might also have attended Protestant services, which were more apt to have hymns and prayers sung in Hawaiian. Kahahawai had had a Catholic funeral service, but when he was finally laid to rest at Puea Cemetery, Reverend Robert Ahuna of the Hoomana Naauao O Hawaii performed the committal service at the gravesite. Speaking to the large crowd in Hawaiian, Reverend Ahuna described Kahahawai's last days as spent in law-abiding innocence: "This man, innocent of what was to take place, went to the judiciary building to report to the court. He knew not that he would be taken out and murdered." Likening Kahahawai and perhaps all Native Hawaiians to Abel, the first son of Adam and Eve, Reverend Ahuna related the story well known to anyone who read the Paipala Hemolele, or Holy Bible. Kahahawai had been struck down by an act of evil, just as the good son, Abel, had been slain by his wicked brother, Cain.

Though Kahahawai's murder was certainly not the first instance of a Native Hawaiian death at the hands of a haole, Reverend Ahuna saw Kahahawai's death as a watershed event: "Within the bounds of our birthplace, such a thing has never been heard of. . . . I call upon the Lord to pass judgment on those who committed this crime."[23] Like other leaders, religious and otherwise, Reverend Ahuna saw the outright lynching of Kahahawai as an unspeakable and shocking crime, one unexpected in the modern era.

The funeral service closed with hymns sung in Hawaiian, such as "Ka Lani Kuʻu Home," or "Angel's Welcome." The largely Native Hawaiian audience also sang the anthem "Hawaiʻi Ponoʻi" and "Aloha ʻOe." Even though the meanings of these Hawaiian-language songs might be lost on audiences that sing them at public gatherings today, it is entirely possible that the Native Hawaiian audience and other individuals fluent in Hawaiian grasped the *kaona*, or hidden meaning, of these songs in 1932. "Hawaiʻi Ponoʻi" was the territory's anthem and is currently the state anthem, but its lyrics are deeply nationalistic and political, calling upon Native Hawaiians to support King Kalākaua (1836–1891), who composed the song in 1874.[24] According to John Charlot, a scholar of Hawaiian music, poetry, and art, "Hawaiʻi Ponoʻi" was a site of resistance that called to mind allegiance to chief, land, and people. Like other Hawaiian cultural forms since contact with the West, the anthem "seemed designed to exploit the gap between Hawaiian and non-Hawaiian understanding."[25]

On the surface "Hawaiʻi Ponoʻi" is a moving *mele* (song) indeed, sung to the melody of "God Save the King." Kalākaua modeled the lyrics on themes found in anthems during Lunalilo's time that used traditional warrior imagery and chiefly honorific terms in calling to mind the reign of Hawaiʻi's first monarch, Kamehameha the Great.

Hawaiʻi ponoʻi,	Hawaiʻi's own,
Nana i kou moʻi,	Look to your king,
Ka lani aliʻi,	The royal chief,
Ke aliʻi.	The chief.
Makua lani e,	Royal Father,
Kamehameha e,	Kamehameha,
Na kaua e pale,	We shall defend
Me ka ihe.	With spears.
Hawaiʻi ponoʻi,	Hawaiʻi's own,
Nana i na aliʻi,	Look to your chiefs,
Na pua muli kou,	The children after you,
Na pokiʻi.	The young.

Hawai'i pono'i,	Hawai'i's own,
E ka lahui e,	O nation,
'O kau hana nui	Your great duty
E ui e.	Strive.[26]

"Aloha 'Oe" is less nationalistic, but the lyrics call to mind the song's famous and accomplished composer, Queen Lili'uokalani (1838–1917).[27] In Hawai'i as in other places, culture and politics were expressed together. More specifically, the singing of *mele* like "Hawai'i Pono'i" and "Aloha 'Oe" was a communal cultural activity that helped to preserve bonds among Native Hawaiians. More than mere songs, these *mele* were modes of storytelling—of handing down and perpetuating the *mo'olelo* of Hawai'i. The monarchs of the previous century, the late Kalākaua and Lili'uokalani, lived on in the minds of Native Hawaiians through *mele*. They and the songs associated with them served as cultural referents, pointing to an alternative, Native Hawaiian politics that predated the existence of the Territory of Hawai'i.

NATIVE HAWAIIAN POLITICS: ELECTORAL, CULTURAL, AND RACIAL

In recent decades social and cultural historians have argued that our notion of the political must be broadened to include activities beyond the ballot box. The nuanced politics expressed through Native Hawaiian *mele* are one example, but there were also numerous electoral campaigning practices that effectively demonstrated how electoral politics was deeply influenced by a careful understanding of modern Native Hawaiian cultural activities. Several Native Hawaiians were prominent in territorial politics, but Native Hawaiians were also a heterogeneous population. As scholars have recognized both in the 1930s and today, Native Hawaiians comprise a diverse population, with pronounced differences between rich and poor. Although Native Hawaiian elites reigned as monarchs in the nineteenth century and have held prominent posts during Hawai'i's history as a territory and a state, larger numbers of working-class Hawaiians have generally experienced difficult social conditions. According to Kekuni Blaisdell, a Native Hawaiian physician and current activist, Native Hawaiians as a group have the shortest life expectancy, low high school and college graduation rates, and some of the highest rates of incarceration among ethnic groups in the islands. All of this is shocking, says Blaisdell, because it takes place "*In our homeland!* So in health, socially, economically, [and] educationally, we're at the bottom—and the situation is getting worse."[28]

In the early twentieth century presses in Honolulu and on the continent were more likely to listen to prominent Native Hawaiians like Abigail Kawananakoa (1882–1945) than to the working poor. Kawananakoa was not a member of the working class, but her visibility as Republican National Committeewoman for the Territory of Hawai'i made her important not only among Native Hawaiian men and women, but also among other island Republicans and the League of Women Voters. Kawananakoa was married to Kalākaua's nephew, Prince David Kawananakoa, and was thus sometimes referred to as "the Princess." Since she was part of a royal Hawaiian family, American tabloids often found her life intriguing enough to publish feature articles about her.[29]

During the Massie case Kawananakoa was vocal in criticizing the ineffectiveness of the territory's legal system. Looking briefly at her life is one way to discuss the diversity among Native Hawaiians and the gradual shift in political orientation that took place in the territory in the 1920s and 1930s. Though Native Hawaiians were treated with much disdain by many haoles, both American merchants and planters and Native Hawaiian leaders had come to see the necessity of forming alliances with one another. Shortly after contact with the West, for example, Kamehameha the Great engaged Isaac Davis and John Young as Western advisors in unifying the island chain in the late eighteenth and early nineteenth centuries.[30] Succeeding monarchs struck occasional partnerships with prominent American missionaries and businessmen in Westernizing their way of life and establishing a strong monarchy system of government. Native Hawaiian groups protested the islands' annexation to the United States, but when it appeared that restoring Queen Lili'uokalani to power was unfeasible, many Native Hawaiians made the best they could of the routes to power that an American system of government and politics made available to them.[31]

Even on the continental United States, newspaper and magazine readers followed news about the royal family in Hawai'i—and through such reports they learned that after Queen Lili'uokalani's death in 1917, Abigail Kawananakoa was one of the few remaining members of royalty, related through blood or marriage, to an heir to the throne. Upon Kawananakoa's death in

1945, a story in the *American Weekly* spent many words describing the lavish
clothes she wore while touring Europe.[32] Whereas the continental press was
often fascinated by the former monarchy in Hawai'i—the only one on U.S.
soil—the local press was more aware of Kawananakoa's potent political power
within the Territory of Hawai'i. As a leader in the Republican Party, her views
also held considerable weight with the territory's delegate to Congress, Victor
Houston.

Kawananakoa formed the Republican Women's League of Hawaii in 1928,
linking herself with other women over the age of twenty-one who had lived
in the islands for at least a year.[33] The league's first meeting was attended by
a large number of Native Hawaiian women, so Kawanankoa enlisted a male
guest, Sam Keliinoi, to translate the speakers' remarks into Hawaiian. Like
other political gatherings in Hawai'i, the meeting ended with a Hawaiian luau
and a program of hula. Hawaiian entertainment during the territorial years
was often used in the service of political campaigning.[34] The general Hawaiian term for this currying of favor for the purpose of politics was known as
ho'omalimali.[35]

Kawananakoa was extremely active in the late 1920s and early 1930s in
defending the rights of Hawai'i residents facing the perils of an unjust government or of Big Five interests that ran counter to the majority of the voting
public. When some officials on the continent advocated restructuring the
territory so that it would be ruled under a commission form of government
headed by the military, Kawananakoa opposed this as well. She was not necessarily a friend of the working class, but she did defend residents of Hawai'i
from what she saw as bad laws and bad decisions.

In this respect Kawananakoa operated as a Native Hawaiian who articulated the discontent that local Hawai'i residents had with laws that bullied
them into continually accepting poor social conditions and poor political
representation. The threat of commission rule was recognized as "a club to
drive laws through a local legislation."[36] According to the *Hawaii Hochi*, "For
years our local leaders in politics and industry have been trying to frighten
the people of Hawaii with threats of a 'Commission form of government.' To
serve their own selfish ends and whip reluctant citizens into line, they have
painted a terrifying picture."[37]

In the spring of 1932 the Big Five became worried about a possible
change in the political status quo. As a result of the Massie case, Representative Frederick Britten of Illinois introduced a bill to Congress suggesting a

commission form of government in Hawai'i that would change the selection process for the governor of the Territory of Hawai'i. Power would be taken away from the Big Five and other business elites. The *Hawaii Hochi* pointed out that haole elites would have the most to lose under the proposed form of government, since the selection process for the chief executive of the territory would take place more in Washington, D.C., than locally. The Britten bill would "absolutely prevent the dictation of appointments by the local coterie of 'big interests.' . . . It would strike a fatal blow at the domination of the local government by our captains of industry."[38]

ANNEXATION: PRODUCING A POLITICAL PREDICAMENT

Annexation significantly altered Hawai'i's demographic and political representation. Becoming part of the United States in 1898 meant two important things. First, Hawai'i was now subject to the same restrictions against immigration from Asia. Second, annexation brought universal male suffrage for those over age twenty-one, and after 1920 these voting rights were extended to women as well.

In the early years of the territory, haole governing elites recognized that they were vastly outnumbered by peoples of color. By 1930 there were 10,503 Native Hawaiian, 9,854 Chinese, and 34,860 Japanese male U.S. citizens of voting age, compared to 22,504 white males of voting age.[39] In order to make up for this numbers deficit, haole elites thought it best to form political alliances with Native Hawaiians, the largest voting group, shortly after annexation. In 1900 Native Hawaiians made up two-thirds of the electorate. Most of them eventually joined ranks with the haole-established Republican Party, favoring it over the Democratic Party. On June 6, 1900, a smaller but significant number of Native Hawaiians established the Native Hawaiian Home Rule Party, which challenged haole dominance.

Despite the fact that many Native Hawaiians and haoles found themselves in the same political party, they were more political partners than friends. As the old saying goes, politics makes strange bedfellows. Working-class Native Hawaiians were more likely to support their own Native Hawaiian candidates than a party that also advanced the interests of white elites. Most did not necessarily support further haole control.

A COMPLEX POLITICS:
THE NATIVE HAWAIIAN–HAOLE
REPUBLICAN ALLIANCE

Though both Native Hawaiian and haole elites established alliances throughout the nineteenth century, the alliance formed in the early part of the twentieth century slowly became complicated by the emergence of a Democratic
Party in Hawai'i. Native Hawaiians were a clear majority of the voters in the
territory; haoles, though powerful, were still a minority as voters. The two
groups formed a political alliance in the Republican Party shortly after annexation in order to counter what they feared would be a large "Oriental vote."[40]
The Chinese population in Hawai'i constituted an old immigrant group that
was prominent financially, but not large enough to strike fear in the hearts of
Republican Native Hawaiians and haoles. In fact, large numbers of successful
Chinese who had moved into the ranks of the middle class joined the Republican Party. Haole elites encouraged Native Hawaiian leaders to be wary of the
growing Japanese population in Hawai'i.

Fears of a large Japanese electorate, however, were unfounded in 1930.
Romanzo Adams determined that although adult Japanese in the territory
outnumbered adults of all other ethnic groups that year, only 16 percent of
the adult Japanese population included U.S. citizens eligible to vote. Six thousand, or 62 percent, of 9,759 eligible Japanese voted in 1930. By comparison,
nearly 17,000, or 84 percent, of 20,130 eligible Native Hawaiians and part-
Native Hawaiians voted that same year. Hawaiians showed more interest in
voting than any other ethnic group—an astounding 99 percent were registered voters.[41] At 72 percent, Japanese had the second lowest percentage of
registered voters, and they certainly did not vote as an "ethnic bloc," as early
forecasters feared they might. In 1930 Japanese did not pose a significant
political threat to Native Hawaiians.

In fact, on a day-to-day basis Japanese and Native Hawaiians worked
closely with one another, especially in working-class neighborhoods of Honolulu such as Kalihi-Pālama and Kaka'ako. Though Japanese in Honolulu
intermarried with other ethnic groups at a lower rate than most, this did not
prevent friendships and working relationships between Japanese and others
of Hawai'i's multiethnic population.[42] In the 1920s and 1930s the Kauluwela Boys themselves were an example of the bonds formed especially among
Native Hawaiian and Japanese American youths. Joseph Kahahawai and

Ben Ahakuelo were Native Hawaiians whose school and playground friends included Horace Ida and David Takai, two Japanese Americans. The fifth member of the accused Kauluwela Boys, Henry Chang, was part-Hawaiian, part-Chinese. Though pure-blooded Native Hawaiians, or *Kānaka Maoli piha*, were on the decline in the early decades of the twentieth century, part-Hawaiians were on the rise. Romanzo Adams would remark later in the 1930s that the proclivity of Native Hawaiians to intermarry perhaps suggested their general openness with other groups.

Native Hawaiians, like all individuals, have a wide range of social relationships. Their elites' political bonds with haole elites did not prevent working-class Native Hawaiians from mingling with "Orientals." The two elite groups formed a political alliance as a means to secure upper-level positions in territorial government. There was some friction over jobs between Native Hawaiians and Japanese, and this was certainly noticeable during the Depression years. But for the most part the bonds of friendship between Native Hawaiians and Japanese remained, especially among the youth populations that shared schooling and recreation activities—activities that their parents' generations had been unable to share. When police detectives questioned Ben Ahakuelo, for example, they thought they could use old ethnic antagonisms to their advantage by attempting to pit the Kauluwela Boys against one another. Detective Watson asked Ahakuelo to remember that he was Hawaiian and to give up his Japanese friends Ida and Takai if they had indeed raped Thalia Massie. Surely these Japanese youths would give him up, a Native Hawaiian, said Watson, if he did not tell his side of the story first. Ahakuelo stood by the truth and his Japanese friends, however, and asserted that neither he nor any of his friends—Native Hawaiian or otherwise—had assaulted Massie in any way.[43]

LOCAL IDENTITY AS RESISTANCE

Instead of reviewing allegiances formed strictly along lines of class or ethnic affiliation, it is also important to consider how historical agents continually negotiate spaces and terrains in the course of everyday lives. During the Massie-Kahahawai case, and throughout the history of the Native Hawaiian Republican alliance with haoles, elite Native Hawaiian individuals and civic organizations looked beyond their class interests. They took up the needs of working-class Native Hawaiians and protested the killing of Joseph

Kahahawai. Native Hawaiian leaders were also perceptive enough to recognize that Kahahawai's death affected all nonwhite locals as well, since it was an assault on the integrity of the territory's judicial system.

Local identity is a fluid, changing, and ongoing process of positioning. Working-class nonwhites during the 1920s and 1930s most often positioned themselves as "local," but they were not the only residents of Hawai'i who did so. Native Hawaiian elites opposed their haole Republican allies when they needed to, seeing themselves as more in line with locals than with *kama'āina* haole elites or *malihini* whites.

Local identity in Hawai'i has strong origins as a class formation, but also, it increasingly became a racialized formation as well. From time to time whites with a long history in Hawai'i could be considered "local," but often they occupied a class position that widely separated their interests from the non-white majority. Skin color became a determinant in whether one was local or not, especially in a growing urban center where personal knowledge of an individual's family history could not always be guaranteed.

Conversely, Native Hawaiians, regardless of class position, were increasingly seen as people of color and thus as locals as well. Throughout the nineteenth century and into the twentieth, an American racial paradigm began taking root and entrenched itself in the islands as Hawai'i became more Americanized. A political economy that put whites in control over nonwhites was firmly in place in Hawai'i by 1930. Even in the years of the closest political alliances between Native Hawaiian and haole elites, white individuals would on occasion reveal the racial ideologies they had learned on the continent. Prince Jonah Kūhiō Kalaniana'ole, a Native Hawaiian Republican delegate to Congress, did his best to represent the Hawaiian people, but he also knew that haole Republicans needed him in order to swing Native Hawaiian votes from the Home Rule Party—a political party that was rapidly gaining the support of Native Hawaiians by promising to work toward returning them to their land. In 1906—a year that was politically frustrating for him—Prince Kūhiō (as he is commonly known and remembered) confided to his friend, John Lane, that behind the gloss of political campaign rhetoric, Republican haole leadership was against him and all Native Hawaiians. Kūhiō told his friend that, at the heart of it, the Republican leadership's attitude was "we don't want no Niggers."[44]

THE FRACTURING OF THE
NATIVE HAWAIIAN–HAOLE
REPUBLICAN ALLIANCE

The political alliance between Native Hawaiian and haole elites in the Republican Party had always been tenuous, and the events of the Massie case made this all the more clear. After Prince Kūhiō's death in 1922, Native Hawaiian elites like his sister-in-law, Abigail Kawananakoa, became valued leaders in the Republican Party who were not afraid to criticize what they saw as inefficient government or patterns of rule that disenfranchised working-class Native Hawaiians and other locals. When prominent whites objected to the mixed jury of the Ala Moana rape case, believing that such a jury comprising Hawaiians, Chinese, Japanese, and Portuguese was ill equipped to carry out justice, Kawananakoa stood by the jury selection procedures of the territory that ensured a jury of local peers from the community. Kawananakoa's only criticism of the jury system was that as of 1931 and 1932, the years of the Ala Moana rape trial and the Kahahawai murder trial, respectively, women were still not allowed on juries in the territory.[45]

Kawananakoa's call for women jurors was a political move that strategically rallied white women to her side. Her actions during the Massie case show the complexities of political alliances. One the one hand, as a Native Hawaiian related to the Hawaiian monarchy, she was supported by Native Hawaiians and looked after them, regardless of their class backgrounds. On the other hand, she was a leader in the Republican Party and the League of Women Voters who rubbed shoulders with and even provided leadership for haole elites in these organizations.

Kawananakoa was critical of the inabilities of the territorial government to ensure proper law enforcement and justice, especially at the close of the Massie case. When Governor Judd eventually commuted the sentences of Grace Fortescue, Thomas Massie, Albert Jones, and Edward Lord for the killing of Joseph Kahahawai, she said publicly that it seemed justice was hard to achieve when men and women of prominence were on trial. On May 2, 1932, the *Honolulu Star-Bulletin* quoted her as saying, "Are we to infer from the governor's act that there are two sets of laws in Hawaii—one for the favored few and another for the people in general?"[46] Kawananakoa, knowing her delicate position between Native Hawaiians and haole elites, chose her words carefully so as not to express this injustice along racial lines. David Kama, a working-class Native Hawaiian and not a public figure, could speak more freely at Kahahawai's funeral and declared, "There is one law for the Hawaiians and another for the white people."[47] Like other Native Hawaiians, Kama recognized and spoke of the racial divide between Hawaiians and whites—and the more general divide between the local population as a whole and haoles, whether *kama'āina* or *malihini*.

A STORY OF RESISTANCE

David Kama delivered the eulogy for Joseph Kahahawai because he shared a similar story of a loved one's death at the hands of a white military man—the killing of a Native Hawaiian by haole prerogative. Newspaper stories also made Native Hawaiians aware that they could be subject to violence because of their skin color. For example, the following story came out of Los Angeles: in February 1932 Maioli and Manuela Kalili, two Native Hawaiian swimmers visiting the city in preparation for the 1932 Olympic Games, were accosted by a gunman, who hit Maioli over the head when he was slow to reveal the whereabouts of a friend. Locals believed that the Kalili brothers had been beaten because they were viewed as Hawaiian "brutes."[48] Native Hawaiians were aware of the stereotypes that circulated about them, and they understood their consequences. Along with being considered "brutes," they were often also characterized as a cheerful people, with physiques that made them adept at sports and possibly hard labor—when they were up to it. Because the dominant American culture believed that Native Hawaiians did not abide by a Protestant work ethic, it produced the stereotype of the "lazy Hawaiian," much in the same way that it deemed Native Americans "lazy Indians" when incommensurable value systems were at odds.[49]

The killing of Joseph Kahahawai brought to mind stories beyond those of Native Hawaiians. Local newspaper readers viewed the beating of his Japanese American friend, Horace Ida, just one month earlier, in December 1931, as yet another instance of haole military personnel terrorizing nonwhites in Hawai'i. The *Hawaii Hochi,* in its editorials, also reminded readers about the Myles Fukunaga case, also known as the "Three Kings Murder Case." Fukunaga, a local Japanese youth, was found guilty of kidnapping and murdering Giles Jamieson, the son of a prominent Honolulu businessman, and was hanged in 1929. The *Hochi,* as well as many locals, knew that because the sensational case involved a white victim and a nonwhite assailant, the wheels of justice turned much more quickly than if the racial backgrounds of the individuals had been switched around. Kawananakoa's words rang true again: the law protected the favored few, but not the masses.

Newspaper editors saw the links among these stories and pointed this out in ethnic papers, particularly the *Hawaii Hochi*. Editorials against the white establishment rarely appeared in the *Honolulu Advertiser,* but the *Star-Bulletin* printed a few, especially after its editors saw Judd's commutation of the Massie-Fortescue party's sentences as a severe weakening of the territorial government. What angered locals most was not necessarily the racist rhetoric of the navy or other continental groups; rather, it was that the territory's own judicial system had succeeded, only to have its executive branch succumb to federal pressure. Locals seemed more upset at the failure of the territorial government to stand up for itself.[50]

Native Hawaiians have been and continue to be a diverse group, separated often by educational background, class affiliation, religion, and political party. What has consistently unified Native Hawaiians since the nineteenth century, however, is a shared history and community of feeling. Native Hawaiians, rich and poor, have been aware of the injustices against their people as a whole since Captain Cook first encountered the islands in 1778. Though a Native Hawaiian elite had often worked hand in hand with Western powers, they were well aware of the effects of haole domination, and like other Native Hawaiians, they harbored feelings of resentment and animosity toward them. Many in the 1920s and 1930s did not fully long for a return to the past, but they certainly recognized that an American political and military hegemony chafed against their traditional ways of life and hampered Native Hawaiian self-government. Native Hawaiian elites like Prince Kūhiō and Abigail Kawananakoa might not have registered their resentment very publicly, but their sentiments against complete haole domination and their defense of Native Hawaiian interests were a thorn in the side of the Republican Party and the Big Five oligarchy that ruled Hawai'i during the territorial years.

Native Hawaiian elites at the outset of the twentieth century forged political alliances with haole elites, but these alliances were always fragile. Among themselves, Native Hawaiians continually recalled their shared pain due to a history of dispossession and oppression. They did not often express open hostility toward haole individuals, but their collective pain during incidents like the killing of Joseph Kahahawai was enough to inform them that their community of interests was generally different from and opposed to those of haole elites. The brief political alliances between Native Hawaiians and haoles in the Republican Party began to break down during the early twentieth century, causing Hawaiians to see more clearly that as a racialized group, they had more in common with working-class immigrants of color. Native Hawaiians, the first people of Hawai'i, recognized and affirmed that they were no doubt locals as well.

4

A CLOSING AND AN OPENING

....

The Massie-Fortescue
Murder Trial

The grand jury of the First Judicial Circuit Court of the Territory of
Hawaii do present that Grace Fortescue, Thomas H. Massie, Edward
J. Lord, and Albert O. Jones . . . did kill and murder one Joseph
Kahahawai Jr., a human being, and then and thereby commit the
crime of murder in the second degree. . . .

—Indictment of the Massie-Fortescue group for second-degree murder,
JANUARY 26, 1932[1]

THE *Territory of Hawaii v. Massie, Fortescue, Lord, and Jones* was the first case
of 1932 to be considered by the grand jury. The prosecutor's office also considered it a small victory that the grand jury ultimately returned a bill of indictment in late January despite the fact that many jurors were employees of
Big Five firms. A national audience followed the Massie case from the fall of
1931 to the spring of 1932, especially during April and the early days of May,
when the Territory of Hawai'i played host to the Massie-Fortescue murder
trial. The trial was held in a territorial courthouse across from 'Iolani Palace in Honolulu, even though some navy officials and members of Congress

attempted to move it to a location on the continent, either the District of
Columbia or in Thomas Massie's home state of Kentucky.[2] This murder trial
was covered by a wider range of media than the rape trial in the fall of 1931,
and since that trial the surprise killing of Joseph Kahahawai in January 1932
served to generate a larger audience of interested followers.

Local audiences in the islands and *malihini* haoles saw the outcome of
the case much differently from those on the "Mainland." This chapter suggests how the curious final events of the Massie-Fortescue murder trial contributed to the ongoing production of local identity in Hawai'i as a cultural
identity. The murder trial's unorthodox legal ending provided closure to the
Massie case for most continental Americans, but it left an open wound for
local audiences. The outcome of the murder trial illustrated and maintained
a boundary between "locals" and "mainlanders" that was crucial to the formation of local identity in Hawai'i.

FROM THE KILLING OF
KAHAHAWAI TO THE
COMMUTATION OF SENTENCES

Shortly after the burial of Joseph Kahahawai in January 1932, both the prosecution and the defense prepared their cases for the matter of the *Territory
of Hawaii v. Massie, Fortescue, Lord, and Jones*.[3] Rear Admiral Stirling had
requested that the four defendants remain in the custody of the U.S. Navy
"for their personal safety." Governor Judd allowed the navy to keep the
Massie-Fortescue group at Pearl Harbor on board the receiving ship USS
Alton. In doing so, Judd actually risked having them whisked away and out
of the jurisdiction of the territory. The navy, however, kept its promise and
put Captain Ward Wortman, Massie's commander, in charge of the four defendants, to serve as their jailor. A grand jury met on January 22 for the first
of two days of testimony. On January 24 the jury, realizing that they might
face the ire of the haole elite, returned "no bill" to Judge Albert M. Cristy.
Cristy refused to accept the jury's decision and instructed them to return on
January 26. That day, the jury hesitated again and returned a "no bill" around
noon, but this time Judge Cristy issued a stern warning, practically instructing them, said some, that returning a bill of indictment was their duty. The
grand jury ultimately indicted Massie, Fortescue, Lord, and Jones with the
required twelve votes.

Cristy came under much public scrutiny for having pressured the jury. Rear Admiral Stirling protested what he saw as tampering on the part of the judge. Stirling reported to the Navy Department in Washington, D.C., that the vote of the grand jury had been twelve to nine in favor of throwing the case out before Cristy sent the grand jury to deliberate again. This preliminary vote was an unconfirmed rumor, and some wondered how Stirling could have received word. Did the navy have an inside source among members of the grand jury? None of the jury seemed to be a spy, but some were worried that the results of their individual votes would be made public. Several men on the grand jury of twenty-one felt that their jobs were on the line, since they were employees of Big Five firms or worked for companies that had contracts with the navy.

One grand jury member, Rudolph Bukeley, resigned from the jury immediately after the Massie-Fortesue group was indicted, in response to Cristy's actions. He wrote to Senator Kenneth McKellar of Tennessee, one of the many southern senators who followed the case, protesting what he viewed as "illegal and intimidating acts of Judge Cristy." Bukeley and other critics of Judge Cristy objected especially to his instructions to the grand jury on January 24, which they believed introduced an unnecessary "race issue" into the case.[4] Cristy's stern warning, made after he received the second "no bill" from the grand jury, was widely quoted in newspapers: "Are you willing to take responsibility for that situation? *You know our racial structure.*"[5]

Defense attorney Clarence Darrow's celebrity status and high fee brought notoriety to the Massie-Fortescue murder trial. Initially the trial date was set for March 10, but the territorial courts had to wait until March 24, when a ship carrying Darrow and his assistant, George Leisure, arrived. The SS *Malolo* was the fastest commuter vessel to and from the continent at the time, but the journey from San Francisco to Honolulu Harbor still required six days.[6] Darrow had agreed to take the case and, according to one account, had accepted a $40,000 retainer.[7] Other sources, such as the *Honolulu Record,* cited $25,000. Based on information from attorneys who had worked with Darrow in the past, Van Slingerland estimates that Darrow's fee was at least $30,000 and that he usually requested half in advance. Rumors also circulated that some of the thirty-five hundred navy men stationed at Pearl Harbor contributed to the Massie-Fortescue defense fund. The navy, however, did not officially help pay for the Massie-Fortescue defense.

THE MASSIE-FORTESCUE
MURDER TRIAL

After the delay caused by Darrow's late arrival to Hawai'i, jury selection for the murder trial was completed on April 7, 1932. Darrow and Leisure were assisted by Honolulu attorney Frank Thompson, who served as co-counsel for the defense.[8] John Kelley, a young Irish American attorney originally from Montana, and his assistant, Barry Ulrich, served as the territorial prosecutors.[9] Though both local and continental newspapers cast Kelley as the underdog, he was not intimidated by the better-known Darrow. Both lawyers questioned potential jurors, and at the end of the selection process twelve jurors were seated: six "Caucasians" (or whites), one of Portuguese descent, two Chinese Americans, one full-blooded Native Hawaiian, and two part-Hawaiians. If we had to categorize these men using the terminology of the islands at the time, we would say that six were haole and six were "local."[10]

Unlike the rape trial months earlier, in this case there was an abundance of material evidence that territorial prosecutors could use to convince the jury that a crime had been committed at Grace Fortescue's rented bungalow on Kolowalu Street in Mānoa Valley.[11] Joseph Kahahawai's clothes had been found rolled in a bundle, a torn strip of his undershirt was discovered in the bungalow's bedroom, where there were bloodstains on the floor, and though the bathtub had been rinsed clean, police found the drain pipe below filled with blood. Though the murder weapon was never definitively identified, Kelley and Ulrich were able to prove that members of the group had access to a .32-caliber Colt automatic and a .32-caliber Iver-Johnson revolver. Vasco Rosa, a clerk at the Diamond Hall sports and hardware supply store, testified that he had sold an Iver-Johnson to Fortescue on December 15 and a Colt automatic two days later to Jones.[12] The coroner determined that a .32-caliber bullet had killed Kahahawai on January 8 by severing the pulmonary artery of his heart. With that blow, Kahahawai's heart stopped and, according to news reports, apparently so did his wristwatch, thus helping to determine the time of death. According to the coroner's report, he bled to death at 9:45 that morning.

COURTROOM DRAMAS
AND STRATEGIES

The Massie-Fortescue murder trial provided numerous opportunities for good stories and entertainment. Clarence Darrow, who had retired a few years earlier and been making money by lecturing at various law schools and other venues, came out of retirement to defend the group. The murder trial was thus an opportunity to see a famous attorney and orator in what might be his last trial. Darrow was masterful in handling the media and aimed to use its various venues to his advantage. He hinted even before the opening of the trial that he would attempt an insanity defense. He made arrangements for prominent psychiatrists (or alienists, as they were sometimes called) to travel to Honolulu so that they could offer their expert opinion on the mental state of Thomas Massie. Darrow knew that newspapers, radio correspondents, and perhaps even a newsreel team would be anxiously waiting to report on his innovative legal strategy. Pleas of insanity were somewhat rare in legal proceedings in the United States up to that time. Darrow planned an even more unusual strategy—the argument that Massie was *temporarily* insane for a period of minutes on the morning of January 8. Darrow clarified to Judge Charles Davis and to court observers beforehand in pretrial hearings and in announcements to the press that Massie would testify to holding the gun, but not to killing Kahahawai: "We will show that the gun was in his hand when the shot was fired but that question as to whether he knew what he was doing at the time is another question."[13]

The trial began on April 11, 1932, four days after jury selection. Each morning of the trial, navy wives lined up in front of the courthouse—some as early as 5:30 a.m.—to wait for a seat. According to the *New York Times,* the trial became "one of the social events of the islands," and women in particular were "offering everything and using every possible bit of influence to get inside the courtroom."[14] When Darrow called Massie to the stand, he practically admitted to killing Joseph Kahahawai. By his account, he pointed the gun at Kahahawai's chest, asked him if he had raped Thalia, and, upon hearing Joe reply, "Yes, we done it," Massie claimed he blacked out.[15]

Massie not only gave his side of the story, but also attempted to provide alleged narratives from the viewpoints of Thalia and Joseph Kahahawai. He even claimed to recall the very words that Kahahawai used moments before his death.

LT. MASSIE: [Kahahawai] sat there trembling and I said, "Now go ahead and tell the whole story. You know your gang was there." And suddenly he said, "Yes, we done it." The last thing I remember was that picture that came into my mind, of my wife when he assaulted her and she prayed for mercy and he answered with a blow that broke her jaw.

DARROW: Did you have a gun in your hand when you were talking to him?

LT. MASSIE: Yes, sir.

DARROW: Do you remember what you did?

LT. MASSIE: No, sir.

DARROW: Do you know what became of the gun?

LT. MASSIE: No, I do not, Mr. Darrow.

DARROW: Do you know what became of you?

LT. MASSIE: No, sir.[16]

Massie's memory was apparently extremely sharp until that point when he conveniently blacked out.[17]

More dramatic than Massie's testimony was that of Thalia when she took the stand on Wednesday, April 20, the twelfth day of the trial.[18] On that day territorial prosecutor Kelley tried to argue that Darrow could not question her on her alleged rape in September because such events were not entirely relevant to the trial at hand. However, on the eighth day of the trial, when Darrow had asked Massie about his wife's ordeal, Kelley objected on the grounds that references to the Ala Moana assault were relevant only if the defense intended to show that the alleged rape drove one of the defendants to insanity.[19] Darrow responded that that was precisely his intent; he confirmed that his strategy was to argue for a verdict of not guilty by reason of insanity. Because of this strategy, the narrative of Thalia Massie's alleged rape could be used in the Massie-Fortescue murder trial and thus was allowed into evidence despite the objections of the territorial prosecutor.

When Thalia Massie took the stand, many of the women in the courtroom applauded her courage to tell her story before such a public audience. Darrow predicted that her appearance would make for a strong emotional appeal and would demonstrate that her ordeal was so horrific that it had caused the momentary derangement of her husband. What made Thalia Massie's testimony in this case different from what she had provided in the earlier Ala Moana rape trial was her addition of an event not mentioned at that time: an abortion in October 1932. Darrow tried to garner as much sympathy for Thalia so that he could gain sympathy for her husband and his co-defendants. Darrow then asked her about Thomas' state of mind.

DARROW: How did Tommie take all this?

THALIA M.: He could not sleep or eat and he got so thin.[20]

Thomas Massie had also mentioned an abortion during his testimony earlier in the trial. He testified that he lost much sleep after Thalia's alleged rape and that it was never out of his mind.

> LT. MASSIE: After Mrs. Massie's mother [Grace Fortescue] came, we knew that an operation was necessary to prevent pregnancy. This had a strange effect on my mind.
> DARROW: Was it done, the operation?
> LT. MASSIE: Yes. I took her to the hospital and Dr. Withington performed the operation.
> DARROW: Did you know, or did she know, that that pregnancy was due to you or not?
> LT. MASSIE: There couldn't be any doubt that it wasn't.[21]

Massie's testimony implied that it was possible that Thalia had been impregnated by one of her alleged rapists. Kelley, interestingly enough, did not attempt to contest Thalia's alleged pregnancy, even though he had in his possession an official copy of the report on her operation at Kapiolani Maternity Hospital signed by Dr. Paul Withington. The document showed that on October 13, 1931, Thalia Massie had indeed had an operation. In an overlap of civilian and military powers, Dr. John E. Porter, a navy lieutenant, served as a consultant to the hospital physician. The hospital report listed the following findings: "Cervix old bilateral tear. Contents of uterus negative. No enlargement." In laypeople's terms, Thalia had not been pregnant at all.[22]

Events before the trial also provided memorable quirks that would linger in the years that followed. For example, days before the trial started, Darrow attempted surfing with the legendary Duke Kahanamoku as a way to work the press and get a feeling for the community of Honolulu.[23] He also spoke out against Prohibition and told the press that he hoped the Volstead Act would be repealed soon, thus making it easier for people to get a drink.[24] Ironically enough, on the eighth day of the trial, after testimony had ended for the day, Darrow apparently took in a bit of local culture and drank too much ʻōkolehao. Not surprisingly, he was unable to appear in court on Friday morning. Judge Davis accommodated Darrow's condition by starting that day's proceedings in the afternoon and calling for a session on Saturday to make up for lost time. On another Saturday, court security had to be tightened after a gun was reportedly seen in the bag of a woman waiting in line. Press photographers took photos of police patting down everyone entering the courtroom that day, including the eminent Clarence Darrow.[25]

One unforgettable courtroom event was the interrogation of Thalia Massie by Kelley. Many in the haole community and on the continent believed that she had been through too much already and should not be subjected to harsh questioning. During her testimony, Kelley asked if she had ever been subjected to a psychological examination. When Thalia replied that she had not, Kelley handed her a sheet of paper that appeared to be a questionnaire she had filled out while enrolled in a psychology course at the University of Hawaiʻi. Thalia promptly tore up the paper while on the stand and burst into tears, creating a scene that newspapers reported on in great detail. Many believed that Kelley's tactics were dastardly and perhaps an ethical breach of the confidentiality between doctor and patient.[26]

Closing arguments were also memorable, with both Darrow and Kelley making their remarks to a packed courtroom. Police armed with machine guns were reportedly on hand as well. Darrow's closing speech lasted for four hours and twenty minutes—so long that Judge Davis called for a break after the first hour and then for a lunch break a couple of hours after that. Darrow spoke of many things, aiming for a dramatic effect that was based on sympathy for the Massie family. Kelley's closing speech, by comparison, was a much shorter, one-hour presentation of logic and reason. In his summation, he also demonstrated his familiarity with local speech patterns. Joseph Kahahawai would not have confessed by saying, "Yes, we done it," as Thomas Massie asserted. It would have been an awkward thing for a Native Hawaiian to say. Instead, and displaying his knowledge of Hawaiʻi Creole English, Kelley suggested that "He would have said 'We do it' or 'We been do it.' That is the Hawaiian vernacular. There is no past tense in the Hawaiian language and they don't use that vernacular, which is common on the mainland."[27] Kelley's remarks were complete by 3:37 p.m. on Wednesday, April 27. At 4:25 p.m. Judge Davis gave instructions to the jury and sent them to deliberate.[28] The decision was now in the hands of twelve men of the Territory of Hawaiʻi.

THE VERDICT

The jury deliberated that afternoon, took a break for dinner, and deliberated further until they were sequestered at the Young Hotel. Jurors were escorted the next morning to the judiciary building but were unable to reach a decision. On the third day, Judge Davis asked jury foreman John Stone if there was any possibility of reaching a verdict soon. Stone surprised quite a few when he said a verdict was possible before long—many had been expecting a hung jury, as in the Ala Moana rape trial. After another half-hour of deliberations, the jury finally reached a verdict. Stone delivered four slips of paper, one for each of the accused, to the court clerk. The judge reviewed the papers and handed them back to the clerk to be read aloud. One by one, the clerk read the same verdict for Thomas Massie, Grace Fortescue, Edward Lord, and Albert Jones: "Guilty of manslaughter. Leniency recommended."[29] The judge set the sentencing date for Friday, May 6, 1932.

WHAT NOW?

John Kelley had defeated the great Clarence Darrow, but now there was some confusion as to what should be done. Territorial officials had agreed that the navy would hold the defendants until the conclusion of the trial, but did "conclusion" mean the reading of the verdict or the sentencing of the convicted? Kelley did not offer a challenge when Captain Wortman stepped forward and escorted the four defendants back to their quarters on the *Alton*.

Governor Judd shocked the press when he announced that the sentencing date would be moved up two days, to Wednesday, May 4. That morning, Judge Davis sentenced all four to the term prescribed by law: "Not more than ten years' imprisonment at hard labor in Oʻahu prison."[30]

In the end, Darrow felt that he had misjudged the jury by not assessing the impact of race. According to Darrow, "The brown section of Hawaii . . . feel that white men get everything but a few offices . . . whites have most of the land and money." Surely a jury of white men would have acquitted his clients. Darrow believed that "the brown members wanted to be fair; there were Chinamen in the jury box, and Japanese, and Hawaiian and mixed bloods; it was not easy to guess what they were thinking about, if anything at all. Obviously, they do not think as we do, about our side of a situation."[31] As Masaji Marumoto would point out decades later, in 1983, Darrow was well off the mark in his assessment of the ethnic backgrounds of the jury: six of the jurors were white, and not one was of Japanese descent. Any of the twelve jurors, for that matter, could have hung the jury with a single vote.[32]

OFF TO JAIL

After the sentencing hearing, Sheriff Gordon Ross took custody of Massie, Fortescue, Lord, and Jones and escorted them out of the courtroom and the judiciary building. Instead of ushering them into a vehicle for transport to the prison, however, Ross led them across the street to the governor's office in ʻIolani Palace. Minutes later, Governor Judd read a statement to the assembled members of the press: "Acting on a petition from [the defendants], their counsel, and also upon recommendations of the jury which convicted them, I hereby announce I have commuted their sentence to one hour, to be served in the custody of the High Sheriff."[33]

ENDING WITH A WOUND

Theon Wright, a Honolulu reporter at the time, believed that Darrow and Leisure had failed to understand the "bitterness that lay behind the Territory's experiences of the past few months. . . . Their contacts in Honolulu, as had been noted, were with the haole elite, the 'leading citizens' and the *malihini haoles* from the Navy. It is doubtful if the underlayer of public sentiment that had festered like a closed wound since the Ala Moana trial was thoroughly understood."[34] In his book, *Rape in Paradise,* Wright also wrote of "a large and angry segment of the people of Honolulu" who did not agree with the reasoning provided by people like Darrow.[35] Furthermore, what solidified local meaning for the Massie case was the repetition and continued emphasis on the "racial issue" by ethnic presses like the *Hawaii Hochi*. Darrow had hoped to play a role in "healing racial wounds," but he showed little understanding of how race relations in Hawaiʻi were much different from those on the continent.

In his epilogue to *Rape in Paradise,* Wright made a special effort to criticize Darrow—a man who had been a personal friend of his father, George Williams Wright, editor of the Japanese- and English-language *Hawaii Hochi*. In recounting a conversation between Darrow and his father after the murder trial, Theon Wright described how George told Darrow that he failed to understand the "racial issue" in the islands. The elder Wright filled Darrow in on the background of Hawai'i, speaking of "the growing disenchantment of the Hawaiian people with the small clique of *kamaaina haoles* that had gained control of the Islands; the political ferment and discontent; and finally, the refusal of the *haole* elite to accept the decision of their own laws and courts in the case of the Ala Moana defendants."[36]

LEGAL ENDINGS, LEGACY BEGINNINGS

Historian and philosopher Hayden White has suggested that the plot of a narrative can impose meaning on historical events by "revealing at the end a structure that was immanent all along."[37] White also believes that the desire for closure in a historical narrative is a demand "for moral meaning, a demand that sequences of real events be assessed as to their significance as elements of a moral drama." It is the closure of the narrative that allows for meaning; without closure, an account of the events as they progressed would be merely a chronicle, a listing of occurrences in sequential order with no clear beginning, middle, and end. Historical narratives have formal coherency and, according to White, reveal "a world that is putatively 'finished,' done with, over, and yet not dissolved, not falling apart." Narratives provide a "completeness and fullness of which we can only imagine, never experience."[38]

The Massie case reached legal closure when the Massie-Fortescue group, though found guilty of killing Native Hawaiian Joseph Kahahawai, was set free. In the early stages of the story and throughout the Massie case, many on the continent and in Hawai'i predicted that in the end no harm would come to the Massie-Fortescue group. Knowing the power available to whites, to the military, and to the federal government, many knew that the Territory of Hawai'i and its local population had little chance of victory. An editorial in the *Nippu Jiji* expressed local sentiments perfectly: "We had a hunch that something like this would happen. After being held informally for an hour, Lt. Massie and the three others were freed. [The] Kahahawai murder case was closed forever."[39]

Although the Massie case ended legally in May 1932, with the commutation of sentences and the departure of the Massie-Fortescue group for the continent,[40] the story would continue for years and decades for the residents of Hawai'i. Hayden White notes that historical narratives can only approximate reality: "In so far as historical stories can be completed, can be given narrative closure, can be shown to have had a plot all along, they give to reality the odor of the ideal." Locals achieved no narrative closure for the case. Instead, the Massie case could now serve as an origins story for local identity—as an example of injustice against working-class peoples of color in the islands. The daily lives of Hawai'i residents, for example, continued on after the spring of 1932. Readers from the continental United States, on the other hand, could shift their attention to other matters since the Massie case, to them, was more of a newspaper story, a serial drama that took place thousands of miles away, instead of a quotidian reality.

According to White, the plot of a historical narrative is always some sort of an "embarrassment": the plot "has to be presented as 'found' in the events rather than put there by narrative techniques."[41] In retellings of the Massie case there are at least two different endings, expected by different audiences. A continental audience closed the case in May 1932 as an interesting story with a tidy completion. These readers could now direct their attention to other news stories like the search for Charles Lindbergh's baby son, who had been kidnapped just before the start of the Massie-Fortescue murder trial.[42] In contrast, local audiences viewed the story as unfinished and whose effects continue to the present day. The suggestion of an unfinished ending functions as a terminating trajectory for the narrative, thus allowing the story to be told as the backdrop for future events. As a story that ends in injustice for the local population, the Massie case narrative can thus be employed as a story about the origins of local identity (as seen by Andrew Lind and as recorded in Eric Yamamoto's senior thesis) or about the delay of statehood by nearly three decades (as remembered in many Hawai'i history texts). By calling the Massie case a tragedy or, as Wright has called it, an event that "will never be forgotten by the dwindling *kamaainas* of Hawaii," the local ending of the narrative is, in fact, no clear ending at all.[43]

Just what did Wright mean when he referred to the dwindling number of *kama'āinas*? He likely was referring to the old-time Native Hawaiians and other locals who were nearing the twilight of their lives by the mid-1960s, when *Rape in Paradise* was published. Some of the key figures in the Massie case would die in the late 1960s and early 1970s. A few local observers like Lawrence Judd and Masaji Marumoto would live into the 1970s and 1980s and would publish their sides of the story. Little did Wright know at the time that the story of the Massie case would live on, having an audience of successive generations.

STORY, MEMORY, HISTORY

Memory was the only means possessed by our ancestors of
preserving historical knowledge; it served them in place of books
and chronicles.

—*David Malo, Native Hawaiian historian,* 1838[1]

Glen Grant was mistaken. I was not at the trial—being part
Hawaiian and working at an insurance company. I was not asked
as a juror—I was questioned at the office the day after the tea
house incident, that was all. My Dad knew Mr. McDuffie, lead
detective, and all the city officials as my Dad was an Auditor with
the Territory.

Glen Grant dramatized the trial of the Massie Case and I found
it most interesting. Should Glen Grant have another showing I
would love to attend, wouldn't you!!?

—*Letter to the author by Miriam Woolsey Reed, Mānoa resident,*
HONOLULU, HAWAIʻI, JUNE 12, 1996

MIRIAM WOOLSEY REED's words in 1996 about the Massie case underscore
common criticisms made about oral history and public history: that people's
memories sometimes fail, or that storytellers like Glen Grant do not always
get the facts straight. Inaccuracies, half-truths, and glitches in the historical
record, however, are also common to written histories based on documentary

sources. Reed's comments also show the degree to which public history can serve as an engaging, communal practice that often reaches a wider audience than academic texts do.

Storytellers, writers, and historians choose to use some sources and not others. The selection of sources, and then their interpretation, produces different perspectives. There is no such thing as objective truth. In telling a concise story, or even in crafting a teaching curriculum, one needs to be selective. In retelling the Massie-Kahahawai case here, for example, I have scaled back on the "true crime" details in order to spend more time discussing the way the case impacted various communities both then and now. I also used sources—many of them oral or even fictionalized forms of popular culture—in order to get at issues of memory and emotion.

How has the Massie case been remembered in the decades since 1931? Unlike the times of precontact Native Hawaiians discussed by David Malo, memory has not been the only means of preserving knowledge about the case. Residents of Hawai'i in the twentieth and twenty-first centuries have instead relied on the overlap and interplay of memory, books, chronicles, video productions, and Web pages in "re-membering," or putting together various details about the case in order to come to a better understanding of it. Considering the forms that these memories have taken, we need to think more seriously about the relationship between oral histories and written sources, between "official" histories and popular, collective memories. Historian John Bodnar, for example, has suggested that public memory "emerges from the intersection of official and vernacular cultural expressions."[2] Modern technological changes have also altered the ways in which memories of the case have been stored and transmitted. Commenting on such media shifts, cultural historian George Lipsitz has noted, "Time, history, and memory become qualitatively different concepts in a world where electronic mass communication is possible."[3] Lipsitz made this comment in the early 1990s, and since then the Internet has become far more developed, giving people worldwide a plethora of information about any topic—at their fingertips and nearly instantaneously.

Historians have recognized issues of "memory" as playing a crucial role in examining the past.[4] In the fields of social history, cultural history, and ethnic studies, for example, scholars have drawn greater attention to the interrelationships among oral history, family history, group history, and national history.[5] In some respects, this interest in "memory" comes from parallel scholarship in modern European history; the interest also seems to stem from works that have been produced by social historians of the United States since the late 1960s that shed light on the experiences of working-class groups.[6]

In the first three decades after 1931 a number of people held firsthand knowledge of the case, since it had happened during their lifetimes. Some Honolulu residents were even more personally familiar with the case because of its impact on friends, relatives, neighbors, and coworkers. There were fewer personal connections to the Massie case beyond the island of Oʻahu, but the residents of neighboring islands were still sensitive to threats to the territorial government posed by federal officials. Their responses to the case were just as vehement as those expressed by Oʻahu residents. One Maui resident, convinced that the Kauluwela Boys were innocent, put it quite simply, but forcefully, in a 1996 interview: "They got the wrong guys!"[7]

In the post–World War II period, some memories are still based on personal connections to the Massie case, but many also draw upon the retelling of the case in newspapers and popular accounts ranging from high school and college history textbooks, television productions like the 1985 CBS miniseries *Blood and Orchids,* and dramatizations like Glen Grant's historical re-enactment of the rape and murder trials. In the eight decades since 1931, very little additional material evidence about the Massie case has come to light—and this is not surprising. The case was one of the most heavily investigated of its time in Hawaiʻi. And yet local audiences continue to ask the question: who *really* raped Thalia Massie? In the 1930s the answer was almost a foregone conclusion for those on the continental United States—like Rear Admiral Yates Stirling Jr., who had a clear opinion of how nonwhite men behaved in the presence of white women. In the early twenty-first century, however, the questions we are inclined to ask have changed: discussions of racial and ethnic relations have become more frequent and nuanced. Individuals are also less likely to make bold public proclamations concerning race and ethnicity.

History is a dialogue between past and present, as well as between here and there—a negotiation between the "unofficial" stories told at the periphery and the "official" ones at the core that are recorded and archived. Were the actions of the territorial and federal governments warranted? Was the lynching of Joseph Kahahawai as popular on the continent as the Hearst papers suggested? Perhaps not, on both accounts: nearly forty years after the trial, in 1970, Governor Judd said that he deeply regretted commuting the sentences of the Massie-Fortescue party. Mere months after she left the islands, even Grace Fortescue indicated that she was sorry for her actions, remarking in 1932, "I sincerely regret the death of Kahahawai. I do not believe in lynch law. I cannot state that too emphatically."[8]

THE 1930S: MAGAZINE ARTICLES
AND THE PINKERTON REPORT

In the years shortly after the case, a few popular and true-crime magazines on the continent cashed in on the recent memories. Grace Fortescue took *Liberty* magazine up on its offer and wrote her version of her "Honolulu Martyrdom."[9] In 1932 Bernarr Macfadden's *True Detective Mysteries* magazine featured a twelve-page article on the Massie case, dubbing the story "Hawaiian Horror."[10] Neither article, however, generated sustained interest in the Massie case on the continent.

In Hawai'i memories of the case persisted in the late 1930s and throughout the 1940s. The buildup and continued presence of the military were constant reminders of the arrogance that the military displayed during the Massie years. During this decade all of the principals in the case, with the exception of Kahahawai, were still alive. Working-class individuals knew about the case through local newspapers or informal networks in the community. The preponderance of Native Hawaiians on the Honolulu police force also ensured that Native Hawaiians and other working-class peoples in urban Honolulu were kept abreast of recent developments in the case.[11] The investigative efforts of both the Richardson Report team and the Pinkerton detectives also seemed to help individuals in Hawai'i to recall the case. The Richardson Report, for example, conducted under the direction of Assistant Attorney General Seth W. Richardson, included interviews with more than two hundred prominent individuals on the status of social conditions in the islands, as well as transcriptions of more than two thousand pages of testimony. Even after the Massie-Fortescue group left the islands in early May 1932, interviewers employed by the Richardson Report team and by the Pinkerton Detective Agency continued to ask questions regarding the Ala Moana assault case and the Massie-Fortescue murder case. The Pinkerton Detective Agency investigated for two and a half months, from June 15 until August 31, 1932. The investigators themselves noted that in the several months since Thalia Massie's alleged rape in September 1931, few new clues had surfaced. Governor Judd had hired the agency in order to resolve any doubts about the case, but he also chose not to publish the Pinkerton Report. It was not until the early 1960s, when books utilizing the report stored at the Hawai'i State Archives were published, that a larger segment of the public knew of its findings.

In reality, the Pinkerton Report did not need to be made public at the time, since there was already a cottage industry of other accounts during the 1930s. Grace Fortescue and Clarence Darrow were quick to cash in on publishing offers, or at least claimed that they merely wanted to present their versions of "what really happened" in the islands. Shortly after Fortescue published her story in *Liberty* magazine, Darrow published his story in a popular periodical of the period, *Scribner's* magazine.[12] By the end of the decade Rear Admiral Yates Stirling Jr. had also managed to publish his own account, devoting a full chapter of his memoir, *Sea Duty* (1939), to the events of the Massie case. His chapter appears to be a revised version of an article he had published in *True Detective* magazine earlier that year.[13]

Stirling's account provides us with some insight into the workings among the elite territorial officials and the navy in Honolulu during the case. Before the events of September 1931, Stirling claimed that he and Governor Judd were friends who even fished together. All that changed, however, when Captain Wortman burst into the admiral's office and announced, "My God, Admiral. Mrs. Massie, the kid bride of Lieutenant Tommie Massie, one of my officers, was criminally assaulted last night about midnight by a gang of half-breed hoodlums on the Ala Moana."[14] From that moment, the events of the Massie case separated the two men, since Stirling believed Thalia Massie's story of rape, whereas Judd was not convinced. Furthermore, Stirling increasingly revealed his racial prejudices in a way that made the territory tense, if not unsafe. He was (and is) well known for stating that upon hearing the news about Thalia, his first inclination was "to seize the brutes and string them up on trees."[15] In short, Stirling advocated swift justice. Judd, as governor of the territory, was more cautious and upheld a thorough investigation and trial.

The Hawaiian Sugar Planters' Association (HSPA) and the Honolulu Chamber of Commerce had also kept in close communication with Governor Judd, especially after the killing of Joseph Kahahawai sharpened attention from the continental U.S. on Hawai'i. In mid-January 1932 the HSPA helped Judd update his files on the two cases by sending him a copy of *Honolulu Advertiser* publisher Lorrin P. Thurston's appraisal of the coverage by the *New York American* and the *New York Mirror,* a copy of Walter Dillingham's telegram to Senator Hiram Bingham III of Connecticut of the Committee on Insular Affairs, and a copy of HSPA president Barnes' wire to territorial Delegate to Congress Victor Houston.[16]

Dillingham wrote his version of the Massie case in the middle of May 1932 in order to minimize the damage that mainland fears might pose to his business interests. His *A Memorandum* was marked "For Private Circulation and Not for Publication" but was widely distributed to newspaper editors on the continent and to members of Congress.[17] Dillingham's Hawaiian Dredging Company depended on navy contracts at Pearl Harbor, and during the Depression years it relied on Public Works Administration projects for revenue.[18]

THE 1940S AND 1950S:
WORLD WAR II AND THE COLD
WAR YEARS

There were few references to the Massie case published in Hawai'i during the 1940s, since accounts of a case highlighting tensions between the local civilian population and the military were not likely to get past military censor boards. The Territory of Hawai'i was under martial law from December 7, 1941, to February 25, 1946, and the military governor was able to prohibit news items related not only to the war, but also to the conduct of the military government. Since the Honolulu police operated during these years under military control, newspapers were denied access to police files and were also forbidden to write about incidents of murder and rape in Honolulu.[19] Helen Pratt's history, *Hawaii, Off-Shore Territory* (1944), which was published for a general audience through Charles Scribner's Sons, is also noticeably silent about the Massie case. It describes the restructuring of law enforcement in Honolulu, for example, without mentioning that it was the Massie case that prompted legislative change.[20]

Published accounts of the case occurred only after the war years and away from Hawai'i's shores. Shortly after World War II, Edwin G. Burrows, an anthropologist and Bishop Museum Research Fellow, published *Hawaiian Americans* (1947) with Yale University Press and noted the friction between locals and the military as seen in "little brawls between Hawaiian youths and service men that were not uncommon at Waikiki during the 1930's." Burrows identified stages in Hawai'i, including the "Growth of Haole Prestige" and "Relief from Haole Dominance." He devoted an entire chapter to "Aggression," defining it as any hostile act or act of speech in response to stress.[21] Assuming that local young men had raped Thalia Massie, he suggested that "[a]ggression against haole dominance may have underlain whatever these young men committed."[22]

By the early 1950s, labor and the radical left in Hawai'i were also using memories of the Massie case as a rallying point. The *Honolulu Record,* established shortly after World War II and edited by Koji Ariyoshi and sometimes identified with the Communist Party in the islands, published a thirty-eight-page pamphlet to show how the territorial government, big business, and the navy often worked against working-class locals. The paper survived for ten years, and anti-communists often linked the *Record* to the International Longshoremen's and Warehousemen's Union (ILWU) as well.[23] John Reinecke was the unnamed author of *The Navy and the Massie-Kahahawai Case* (1951), whose subtitle called the twenty-five-cent pamphlet "A Timely Account of a Dark Page in Hawaiian History Worthy of Study." The pamphlet identified the case as a symbol of "a double standard of justice—one standard for the well-connected haole and another standard for the non-white generally."[24] It made use of political cartoons drawn in 1932 by Bill Moran of the *Hawaii Hochi.* It focused most of its ire at inflammatory remarks made by Rear Admiral Yates Stirling Jr., but it also pointed fingers at the *Star-Bulletin,* an establishment newspaper. According to the pamphlet, in 1951 the newspaper argued "contemptuously of the popular demand for mercy in the Majors-Palakiko case"—one that was similar to the Massie case in that the alleged assailants, James Majors and John Palakiko, were young men of color and the victim, Therese Wilder, was white.[25] It also reminded Japanese Americans that the *Star-Bulletin* had sided with "the clamor of upper-class haoles for vengeance in the Fukunaga case of 1928–1929," which involved the kidnapping and murder of a ten-year-old white boy named Gill Jamieson by Myles Fukunaga, a nineteen-year-old Japanese American.[26]

The pamphlet also called attention to how Lorrin Thurston had convened a meeting of the Honolulu Chamber of Commerce in order to respond to Washington's attempts to place a commission form of government in control. In arguing against such a government maneuver, Walter F. Dillingham addressed the chamber, urging them to pressure Governor Judd into reorganizing the police department in January 1932. Before the end of the month, Chamber of Commerce directors were able to persuade Judd to set up a new police commission with five prominent businessmen and Charles F. Weeber, Dillingham's secretary, as acting chief of police.[27] In short, Reinecke's

The Navy and the Massie-Kahahawai Case warned locals to be wary of the military, the territorial government, the establishment press, and big business.

THE 1960S: TRUE-CRIME BOOKS

In 1966 Harper and Row published Peter Van Slingerland's *Something Terrible Has Happened,* Hawthorne Books published Theon Wright's *Rape in Paradise,* and Bantam Books published Peter Packer and Bob Thomas' *The Massie Case.*[28] Honolulu journalist Cobey Black was slated to publish another book on the Massie case, *The Unwritten Law,* with Random House later in 1966, but it was not published because of the three books already on the market that year.

Why three books simultaneously appeared on the Massie case more than thirty years after the fact is unclear. Some have speculated that the Pinkerton Report had been withheld from the public until the early 1960s, but John Reinecke had had access to the Pinkerton Report as early as 1951 for his *Honolulu Record* pamphlet. The rumor might have originated from Reinecke's estimation that the report was suppressed; all he had said in 1951 was that the report had never been published and that "[u]nknown to the general public, it reposes in the [Hawai'i] Archives."[29] As of 2007 the Pinkerton Report has been readily available to the public, printed and shelved in the University of Hawai'i's Hamilton Library.[30]

All three of the 1966 true-crime books made extensive use of the Pinkerton Report in retelling the Massie case, and they differ very little in their accounts. Wright's *Rape in Paradise* shows the greatest familiarity with Honolulu, since Wright was a Honolulu newspaper reporter, and his father, George Williams Wright, was at one time the editor of the Japanese community's paper, the *Hawaii Hochi.* Clarence Darrow and the Wrights were family friends for nearly three generations. In 1966 Theon, however, did not hesitate to criticize Darrow for listening "to the *haole* elite, the Dillinghams, the Castles, the Cookes, who did not like to admit the existence of a 'racial issue,' probably because they had helped create it."[31]

Van Slingerland, from rural Patterson, New York, was less familiar with Honolulu, but that did not stop him from being as critical of the navy, territorial officials, and the Massie-Fortescue group as Wright had been. Van Slingerland's *Something Terrible Has Happened* differs from Wright's book by suggesting that Albert "Deacon" Jones—not Thomas Massie—shot Kahahawai. In an interview Van Slingerland conducted, Jones confessed:

A [JONES]: I shot him.

Q [VAN SLINGERLAND]: *You* shot him?

A: You're God damn right I did.[32]

More than three decades had passed and yet the Massie case continued to be a compelling narrative. Packer and Thomas' *The Massie Case* was even translated into Japanese when it was reprinted by Bantam Books in the 1980s. Aiming to benefit from the publicity of another book, it was billed as "The sensational *true* story behind the novel *Blood and Orchids* [1983]."[33]

Over the years, Honolulu newspapers published occasional stories on the whereabouts of the Massie case principals. In early 1950, newspapers in Hawai'i reported that Thalia Massie Bell, then aged forty and residing in Los Angeles, had been arrested for having "gone berserk" and allegedly attacking her pregnant landlady.[34] Massie then moved to Arizona, enrolled as a student at the University of Arizona, and in 1953 married a fellow student twenty-one years her junior. After the marriage ended in divorce two years later, she moved to West Palm Beach, Florida, where her mother had settled. On July 2, 1963, Thalia Massie died in bed at her apartment of what the coroner called "an accidental overdose of barbiturates."[35]

Wright assessed the timeliness of retelling the Massie case narrative in the 1960s: "In a very direct way, it was a capsule prototype of America today, the throes of racial disturbances that have marred our concept of human freedom and may have shattered the faith of many people in democratic processes." He did not think that Honolulu in the 1930s was entirely like "a Selma, Alabama, in the 1960s" in terms of race relations. Nevertheless, Wright thought that the United States could learn from events like the Massie case and what happens to a society when it is "under the control and guidance of a small group of self-appointed 'elite' or 'supremacists.'"[36]

THE LATE 1960S AND EARLY 1970S: PRINCIPALS IN THE CASE BREAK THEIR SILENCE

Shortly after the true-crime books on the Massie case were published, Ben Ahakuelo became the first and only of the Kauluwela Boys to grant a newspaper interview. Ahakuelo spoke with the *Honolulu Star-Bulletin* when his son, Arthur, was sentenced to a ten-year prison term for killing his wife. He said that he read one of the books about the case and had not cared for it much. He also remembered much intimidation. Upon his arrest at football practice, for example, he was taken to the police station, where he saw "all the brass from the Navy." Furthermore, at the Ala Moana assault trial, "all the big guys in town—the guys working for the big firms—came and sat in the court and stared at the jury. . . . What they were saying to the jurors with their eyes was that, 'If this [*sic*] things doesn't come out the right way you are going to get fired.'"[37]

Two years later, in 1970, Governor Judd published his memoirs, and he included an extensive chapter on the Massie case, since it was perhaps the most memorable event during his years as governor. In newspaper interviews Judd explained how different Hawai'i was as a territory than as a state. Governors during the territorial years were appointed by the president; the territory also fell under the jurisdiction of the Department of the Interior. Above all else, during the buildup for a possible war in the Pacific, the U.S. Navy was highly influential. The Pearl Harbor command exerted pressure on the governor directly and indirectly. The commutation of the Massie-Fortescue group's sentences was a compromise: the party was still guilty, but it could leave Hawai'i.

THE 1970S AND 1980S: THE RISE OF ETHNIC STUDIES IN HAWAI'I, "OUR HISTORY, OUR WAY"

Locals born after the 1930s often learned about the Massie case when it became an established part of educational curricula in the State of Hawai'i. Beginning in 1970, with the establishment of ethnic studies courses at the University of Hawai'i, the events of the Massie case were taught with some regularity in courses on the general history of modern Hawai'i or in ethnic studies and American studies courses.

The early 1970s also witnessed the conflux of two overlapping social movements: the beginnings of the often-termed Hawaiian Renaissance among Native Hawaiians and other concerned locals, and a statewide political initiative to limit the numbers of outside arrivals from abroad and even the continental United States. Both movements assisted in the production of a kind of localism in Hawai'i whereby indigenous Native Hawaiians and the descendants of generations of plantation workers sought to distinguish themselves from non-Hawaiʻi residents and visitors. By the early 1980s this sort of localism had also come to include a movement against real estate investments from Japan.[38]

Anti-Japan sentiment, however, seemed to have little impact in creating anti-Japanese American hostilities in Hawaiʻi. Japanese American–experience courses gained popularity and often featured the Massie case due to the use of Dennis Ogawa's *Jan Ken Po: The World of Hawaii's Japanese Americans* (1973) and Roland Kotani's *The Japanese in Hawaii: A Century of Struggle* (1985), both of which devote extensive sections of text to the case.[39] Ogawa and Kotani, who taught American studies and ethnic studies courses, respectively, at the University of Hawaiʻi, present the Massie case in their books after an extensive discussion of the Fukunaga case of 1928–1929.

The Ogawa and Kotani books included the Massie case because it involved Japanese American defendants Horace Ida and David Takai, several Japanese American witnesses called to the stand, and Japanese American lawyers such as Masaji Marumoto, who was one of the first persons of Asian descent admitted to the bar in the Territory of Hawaiʻi. The Japanese American press also continued to serve the islands as an alternative to the major *Honolulu Advertiser* and *Honolulu Star-Bulletin* news dailies. Readers of all ethnic backgrounds turned to the English-language sections of the *Hawaii Hochi* and *Nippu Jiji* for incisive political commentary.

Individuals in Hawaiʻi have also informally educated themselves about the Massie case in order to make sense of their present situation or to teach newcomers to the islands about race relations. In the early 1980s, while working for the Protect Kahoʻolawe ʻOhana group, Kuʻumeaaloha Gomes helped facilitate women's groups' meetings in the hopes of minimizing tensions between civilian and military wives on the Waiʻanae coast of Oʻahu. She retold the story of the Massie case to women at the Lualualei military installation in order to explain how there was a historical basis for the animosity locals had (and still have) for the military presence in the islands. Her version is easily summarized in two sentences: "There was a navy wife who was raped and she accused five local men. One of them got killed."[40] She also, however, retold one of the many local versions of the story, indicating that Thalia Massie had accused the local young men in order to cover up an affair she was having with another naval officer: "At the hearing it was found out that she had been having an affair and wanted to cover it up because she got beaten up. So she blamed the five men. It just erupted into a big thing with the president of the

U.S. involved. The military was very, very racist. So I explained that case to them [the wives at the Lualualei military installation]."[41]

Ku'umeaaloha Gomes' belief that Thalia Massie was having an affair might have stemmed from long-standing rumors circulated during the 1930s, from the account given in Norman Katov's fictional *Blood and Orchids* (1983), or from the 1986 television miniseries by the same name based on Katov's novel. What is more readily confirmed is that Gomes recognized the need to tell the story to those she believed needed to hear it. She was able to explain to military wives in the early 1980s how an event that occurred decades ago still had a significant impact on the ways that locals felt about the military presence in Hawai'i. In retelling the story to military members residing in Wai'anae—a rural community with large numbers of Native Hawaiians and perennial friction with the military over land use—Gomes emphasized how Native Hawaiian locals in particular had a history of conflict with the military.

Gomes said that after telling the story of the Massie case and linking it to the U.S. military's involvement in using Kaho'olawe and other islands in the Pacific as practice bombing sites, the military wives were astounded. They told her that they had been taught by military brass to be wary of people like her. The women explained their fears, saying things like, "Well, we're really afraid of you. We're told by the commander that Hawaiians hate white people and that you're going to beat up our kids and you're going to beat us up, and we can't go down to the town here in Wai'anae because you hate us." Gomes explained the history of the military in Hawai'i via the Massie case in order to show how "[t]hese are the kinds of things that shape peoples' attitudes and they get really angered, but it doesn't mean that they hate you." Gomes also believed that her remarks on the Massie case and military bombings quickly got her silenced. A woman in uniform who had been appointed by the commander to keep tabs on Gomes stood up during the meeting and told her, "You have five minutes to get off this base. You are giving out confidential information and conducting subversive activity."[42]

Gomes left the Lualualei military base but responded that the information she had shared with the military wives was in no way secret. Because the Massie case had involved the military and the delicate question of the rape of a white woman by nonwhites, it has often been shrouded in some degree of secrecy. Nearly all records concerning the case, however, are readily available to the public via the Hawai'i State Archives and the National Archives and Records Administration branch in San Bruno, California, that holds information about Hawai'i's territorial years. The true-crime books written during the 1960s are public knowledge, as are the newspaper articles that appeared on a nearly daily basis from September 1931 to May 1932. Critics see the Massie case as having the potential to create conflict, while people like Kuʻumeaaloha Gomes believe that retelling the story can prevent future misunderstandings.

In the late 1970s and early 1980s the *Honolulu Star-Bulletin* ran a series of articles describing life in pre–World War II Hawai'i.[43] For example, a 1981 article by Lois Taylor revisited the events fifty years after the alleged rape of Thalia Massie. In a letter to the editor a week later, reader Chris Urago questioned the "judiciousness of unearthing once again the Massie case" and thought it best to "bury this chestnut."[44] The *Star-Bulletin* did not respond directly, instead featuring a letter written by none other than John E. Reinecke, author of the 1951 pamphlet *The Navy and the Massie-Kahahawai Case*. Reinecke urged readers to see the case not simply as "an interesting crime story," but as a part of Hawai'i's history that could "no more be stowed away in the closet, than, for example, the overthrow of the [Native Hawaiian] monarchy."[45] Reinecke outlined several lessons to be learned from the Massie case: it was the first time that "the people of Hawaii were brought up flatly and traumatically against the power of American racialism, reinforced by ignorance of Hawaii"; it showed how precarious political liberties were without statehood; and it revealed the racism of the navy, the power of the press in expressing and intensifying racist feelings on the continent, and the degree to which members of Congress could be influenced by such media coverage. In closing his letter, Reinecke also pointed out that "part of the local haole community, the most conspicuous individual being Walter F. Dillingham, accepted Thalia Massie's version of the affair and openly displayed support of the Massies."[46] This concluding sentence warned locals to be wary not only of the military and the "Mainland," but also the haole elite at home.

In 1980 a curriculum team at the University of Hawai'i chose to include the history of the Massie case in its *The Shaping of Modern Hawaiian History*—a multivolume series complete with a teacher's manual that has since been condensed into a one-volume textbook for high schools and republished in 1989 and 1991. The Massie case is presented largely as an event after which continental audiences formed negative opinions about Hawai'i and its multiracial population, thereby slowing the territory's admission to statehood. The treatment is extensive, taking up a total of nine pages in the

1991 edition, and it involves a summary of the case, three activities, two question sets, and three additional activities. In a lesson designed to cover two class periods, students are to read a summary of the Massie case (a *Honolulu Star-Bulletin* story written in 1981) and then read a series of continental newspaper editorials from the 1930s that are extremely critical of Hawai'i.[47] The stated goals of the lesson plan "Hawaii on Trial" are:

1. To explore the significance of the Massie case in the growth of pro-statehood feelings in Hawaii
2. To examine the effects of the case on mainland attitudes towards Hawaii and its multiracial population
3. To understand some disadvantages of territorial status which contributed to Hawaii's desire to become a state.[48]

According to the teacher's manual, "Specific details related to the guilt or innocence of the parties involved were purposely not included since the aim of this lesson is to examine the effects of the trial on the statehood movement."[49] (If students wanted to read more about the events of 1931–1932, the 1980 teacher's manual suggested the Pinkerton Report for "the most comprehensive account of the case," though the report was available at the time only at the Hawai'i State Archives.) Teachers are encouraged to focus discussion on the larger social and political issues surrounding the case, namely: "a. the racial implications; b. relations between the military and civilian populations; c. the ability of the territorial government to handle criminal acts and administer justice."[50]

The teacher's manual itself represents the case as largely one of opposition between local and nonlocal population groups. The manual encourages teachers to ask questions that will prompt students to draw out these issues from the Massie case on their own. Students are asked to consider the ethnicity of the defendants and jury members of both trials and to predict "possible controversies" that could arise from such situations. Students are also asked to draw parallels to any current social tensions in Hawai'i: "What sector of the community did the defendants in the rape case represent? *(local residents)* How about in the trial for the murder of Kahahawai? *(military personnel)* Do situations like this still happen today? Give some examples. How would you describe relations between the military and the local population in Hawaii?"[51] This lesson plan reinforces the Massie case narrative as one of locals versus nonlocals. The last activity asks students to put themselves in Governor Judd's shoes: would they have commuted the sentences of the Massie-Fortescue group as Judd had done in 1932?

In the mid-1980s interest in the Massie case took another turn when *Blood and Orchids* (1986) was filmed in Honolulu.[52] The shooting of the four-hour CBS television miniseries brought about renewed interest in the details of the case, once again causing audiences to question who indeed had raped Thalia Massie on the night of September 12, 1931. Viewers of the miniseries needed to separate fact from fiction, since it was based not on the Massie case itself, but on the novelization of the events provided by Norman Katov's popular novel of the same name, published a few years earlier. Certain elements were weaved in for dramatic purposes—namely a story line involving a love affair between Honolulu detective Curt Maddox (played by Kris Kristofferson) and Leonore Bergman (played by Sean Young), the young wife of the elder lawyer hired by the wealthy Murdoch-Ashley group. The ending of the miniseries was also one of dramatic justice: the murderers of the Native Hawaiian are forced to serve many years of hard labor at Oʻahu Prison.[53]

The miniseries was also a coup for the local population in another way: Honolulu newspapers celebrated the fact that local actors played not only extras on the set, but also key characters. *Honolulu Advertiser* entertainment editor Wayne Harada encouraged viewers to look for familiar faces, joking in Hawaiʻi Creole English, "Could be your neighbor, brah."[54] Forty-three of sixty-three roles were cast in Hawaiʻi. Three of the four actors who played the Kauluwela Boys were also products of local community theaters.[55] Native Hawaiian actor Elizabeth Lindsey, well-known as a former Miss Hawaiʻi, played a prominent role as the sister of one of the defendants accused of raping Hester Murdoch, the Thalia Massie character (played by Madeline Stowe).[56] Lindsey told a *Star-Bulletin* reporter, "I remember growing up, listening to my parents and their friends talking about the real case. There was a very real sense of futility, anger, and resentment because it was never fully resolved."[57]

This miniseries now serves as a reference point for locals who are too young to have firsthand memories of the Massie case. Like other television productions, matters of guilt and innocence are much more clear-cut than in real life. Hester Murdoch leaves a party early in order to engage in a dalliance with her husband's naval officer friend on the beach, and it is he who badly beats her. The four innocent local boys acted as good Samaritans, but were unjustly accused of rape, having had the misfortune of encountering Hester and transporting her to the hospital. Later, when they are tried in court, a jury of the local population is unable to reach a verdict and, as in the real Massie case, the trial ends in mistrial. Before the court is adjourned, however, an enraged Lieutenant Murdoch shoots the Native Hawaiian defendant John Liluohe in the courtroom, for all to see. In the real case the Massie-Fortescue group was caught red-handed while trying to dispose of Joseph Kahahawai's body; in *Blood and Orchids* the matter is even more clear-cut: an entire courtroom witnesses the murder. Mrs. Murdoch also vindicates the young men by screaming, "No, they didn't do it! They were innocent!"

Thus justice is finally achieved in *Blood and Orchids*. Furthermore, a couple of monologues at the conclusion serve to mark the fictionalized Murdoch rape case as a turning point in the history of Hawai'i. Lawman Curt Maddox denounces Hester Murdoch's mother, Mrs. Doris Ashley, who happened to be a wealthy sugar plantation mistress: "You built the territory so you figured you owned it and the people on it. . . . But that's ending. You can't kill people, and you can't whip 'em, and you can't treat human beings like they're not human—and that's what you've been doing to these people since you stole this land from the people who founded it." Mrs. Ashley and her daughter are then whisked away to jail, charged with perjury and conspiracy to obstruct justice.

The production ends with a speech by Princess Luahine, played by Haunani Minn. The princess, loosely based on Abigail Kawananakoa, also seems to represent Queen Lili'uokalani, who was overthrown in 1893 and jailed. However, unlike Lili'uokalani, who died in 1917, the fictional Princess Luahine tells the four freed local youths that she has survived to see a victory for her people: "You don't know it but something historic happened. . . . I lived long enough to see a jury find a United States Navy officer guilty of a crime in *this* Territory. And yesterday I heard a judge sentence that Navy officer to ten years in prison." She then goes on to instruct the young men to make something of themselves, like the local Japanese lawyer who had represented them. Pointing to the lawyer, she says, "If he can do it, you can do it." Her words of encouragement seem to foreshadow the emergence of middle-class, professional locals in the decades after World War II.

STORYTELLER GLEN GRANT
AND POPULAR HISTORY

The late Glen Grant, who came to Hawai'i in the late 1960s, started a night tour of the Massie case in the late 1980s for tourists and local residents. At the height of its popularity, Grant gave tours once a month for nine years, from 1988 to December 1996. The tour was not without its minor controversies: when a staffer at the Judiciary History Center objected to it, Grant lost access to a courtroom in Aliʻiōlani Hale. Judge James Burns, however, allowed the use of his courtroom, the very one that was used in the original rape and murder trials of 1931 and 1932.[58]

Grant's tour was three hours long, and even he was surprised that, despite the length, "people haven't skipped out in the middle of it because they were bored." In those nine years, several locals volunteered their own stories, telling how they either remembered the case or how their relatives in the Honolulu Police Department had worked on the case. Members of the Ahakuelo family have taken the tour, as has Miriam Woolsey Reed, a Native Hawaiian woman and resident of Mānoa who was at the Ala Wai Inn on the night Thalia Massie was there.[59] Deena Ahakuelo, a grandniece of Ben Ahakuelo, said that it was not until her adult years that she heard "the family lore" about her granduncle: it was hard to talk about his family, since two of his sons had been in trouble with the law. She has said, however, that the family "feels vindicated" since Glen Grant's tour and a series of books have shown that Ben and his local comrades were most likely not Thalia Massie's assailants.[60]

Originally the Massie tour was part of a general history series that Grant started in 1986. It was part of Kapiʻolani Community College's Interpret Hawaiʻi Program—a project designed to foster links between the community and the college. The Massie tour was started as an academic outreach project, but Grant later developed it for his private company, Honolulu Tour Walks, which he had started with Arnold Hiura in the 1990s. The tour was largely educational, and at seven dollars per person it was not a mass commercial venture.[61]

THE 1990S AND THE TWENTY-FIRST CENTURY: WHERE AND WHEN I ENTER

And now I can tell you more about my story—about how my account relates to the larger local story.[62] I am taking the risk of telling you too much about myself so that you can consider how my relationship to this story—this history—has helped to shape my retelling of the Massie-Kahahawai case here. In telling a personal story that is more immediately linked to the present, I am

treading on terrain that professional academic historians are often not comfortable covering. Cultural historian George Lipsitz might characterize my
story as a kind of countermemory—"a way of remembering and forgetting
that starts with the local, the immediate, and the personal."[63] Locals focus on
events like the Massie case—a localized experience of oppression—in order
to reframe a dominant narrative of history that previously excluded their experience. As I mentioned at the outset of this book, I started looking into
the case in the early 1990s, while reading more and more about Hawai'i's
territorial years. I kept coming across the Massie case and was surprised that
I had not heard much about it before, despite the widespread attention that
newspapers in Hawai'i and the continental U.S. had given it in 1931–1932. I
researched the case more thoroughly in the mid- to late 1990s, flying back to
Honolulu when time and funding allowed for it.

In the 1990s, Honolulu-based Mutual Publishing reprinted affordable
paperback versions of Theon Wright's *Rape in Paradise* with an introduction
to the original 1966 hardcover edition published by Hawthorn Books. It became readily available in new and used bookstores that catered to both local
and tourist populations, thus introducing the Massie case to new generations
of readers. Once, in 1997, when I was on a flight from Honolulu to Los Angeles, I saw that the woman seated next to me—a teacher at a community
college in California—was carrying *Rape in Paradise* as her reading material
for the trip. She told me that she had recently seen a rebroadcast of *Blood
and Orchids* on the Lifetime Channel, and a local bookseller on O'ahu had
referred her to Wright's book.

On the continental U.S. there was a revival of interest in the case from
the late twentieth century onward—mainly from a true-crime perspective. In
1996 Max Allan Collins based his historical crime novel, *Damned in Paradise,*
on the Massie case, placing his detective, Nathan Heller, alongside the real-life
lawyers of the case, Clarence Darrow and his assistant, George Leisure.[64] In
1997 and 1998 the Lifetime Channel—owned by the Hearst Corporation and
known for tailoring its programming to women viewers—rebroadcast *Blood
and Orchids.* Those on the continent, however, were not necessarily likely to
know that the miniseries was based on a real incident. Back in 1986, for example, a *Honolulu Star-Bulletin* staff writer was disappointed when the show
"didn't exactly get raves from Mainland critics—*People* magazine, in fact,
called it 'pure hulabooey.'"[65]

In Hawai'i viewers were more likely to remember and draw connections to the Massie case. The narrative has even been used as a litmus test for local identity and allegiance to the people of Hawai'i in recent years. When debates on renaming Porteus Hall, the social sciences building of the University of Hawai'i at Mānoa, arose in 1997 and 1998, for example, Elizabeth Porteus attempted to defend the honor of her late father-in-law by saying that Professor Stanley Porteus was a "pro-Hawaiian witness in the Massie case" and a supporter of statehood.[66] Beverly Keever, a member of the university president's commission on diversity, refuted Porteus' claim by researching the microfilmed transcripts and indexing materials of the murder trial. Keever found no testimony by Dr. Porteus and criticized his work "because it provided the supposedly scientific framework that justified and perpetuated the superiority of the white race at the top of a hierarchy of other races."[67] The lengths to which people like Beverly Keever are willing to research and retell the case are testimony to the vitality of the Massie case narrative.

When I initially completed this study as a dissertation in 1999, I was finishing up one year of teaching in California and then moving to Arizona—in both cases to teach in academic programs that focused on Asian American and Pacific Islander American experiences. Many of the students and community members I worked with had ties to Hawai'i, being there only to attend school or having relatives back in the islands. I mention these details about moving back and forth in order to shed light on why, in writing this book, I have sought to understand better the historical and contemporary differences between Hawai'i and the continental United States.

By the beginning of the twenty-first century there had been a decade's worth of more widespread, popular reflection on the history of Hawai'i more generally. In the fall of 2001 David Stannard put out a call for stories about the Massie case in the *Honolulu Advertiser,* because he was starting research for his book.[68] I was still teaching in Arizona at the time, but I came back regularly to carry out research and visit family.

In 2003 I spent much of the summer attending a National Endowment for the Humanities program on reimagining the indigenous Pacific. It was during this summer that I got to spend extended time with University of Hawai'i scholars.[69] I was encouraged to see things from the viewpoints of Hawai'i and other places in the Pacific. That summer I was also able to talk to Stannard extensively on the phone regarding our research and writing about the Massie case. We talked, too, about helping filmmaker Mark Zwonitzer in creating the *Massie Affair* documentary for WGBH Boston's American

Experience series. (As Stannard and I have openly admitted, we were initially wary of Zwonitzer, and perhaps also of each other.) Stannard and I ultimately served as consultants on the documentary.[70] Stannard and Cobey Black, author of *Hawaii Scandal*, served as on-camera experts about the case, and University of Hawai'i Hawaiian studies professors Haunani-Kay Trask and Kanalu Young also provided on-camera commentary. The documentary also featured people who remembered the case from the 1930s firsthand, notably Ah Quon McElrath, a University of Hawai'i regent at the time and a long-time supporter of the university's Ethnic Studies Department.

Cobey Black had worked on her book for many more years than Stannard and I had. She started in the 1960s and then shelved the project when three books came out in 1966; after Norman Katov published his novel *Blood and Orchids* in 1983, Black again found it difficult to find a publisher.[71] In the end she was able to complete her book and publish with a Hawai'i-based publisher, Island Heritage, in 2002. Black also had the unique distinction, when she was a youngster, of having met Thalia Massie. (When we talked to each other in 2010, Black corrected me and said that Mrs. Massie's name was pronounced "THAY-lia.") Black's parents and Thalia's parents had known each other in navy circles. For this reason, her book is very strong on East Coast details.

In 2004 Dennis Carroll, a playwright and chair of the University of Hawai'i Theatre and Dance Department finally produced his play, *Massie/Kahahawai*. Carroll had written the play in the late 1960s and early 1970s, and instead of using his own words to summarize the events of the case, he took a different approach: he compiled and arranged verbatim quotes from police reports and newspaper accounts in order to characterize Honolulu in the early 1930s. In the 1970s *Massie/Kahahawai* was read through once with University of Hawai'i student actors for a conference in Honolulu, but it was never fully performed on stage because Thomas Massie, still alive and well at the time and residing in San Diego, might have sued if it were produced. Carroll had been warned by Peter Van Slingerland, author of *Something Terrible Has Happened*, who had been threatened earlier with a lawsuit by Massie. Carroll did not want to be seen as cowardly, but he also did not want to put student actors at risk legally. He wound up putting the play in the "proverbial desk drawer," where it lay dormant for three decades.[72] Carroll told me that according to Van Slingerland, Thomas Massie objected to any sort of dramatic presentation of the case.[73] He also told reporter John Berger that he approached the story as "trial as ritual" and that he used a style that was "a cross between Brecht and Artaud."[74]

Carroll's play had extra showings and sold-out performances. I attended in January 2004 along with my grandmother and mother-in-law, and fellow audience members that afternoon included English and political science professors from the university.[75] The play expressed an imagined local identity in its depiction of 1930s Honolulu, but it also focused on how the ordeal was a tragedy for Thalia Massie; at one point, Thalia is portrayed as a puppet, maneuvered by other cast members.[76]

The play generated discussion in a series of panels sponsored by the University of Hawaiʻi's Center for Biographical Research and by the Hawaiʻi Humanities Council. The forums were held at the Judiciary History Center at Aliʻiōlani Hale; in fact, they were held in the very courtroom that the Massie case trials had been conducted in 1931 and 1932. I wrote one of the essays in the readers' guide and supplied a bibliography for theatergoers who wanted to read more about the case. I even listed primary source documents of which casual readers of the 1966 books were unaware. On my panel in January 2004 I sat alongside Ah Quon McElrath and Dennis Carroll. In the audience were family members of some of the jurors of the trials, such as Kekuni Blaisdell, a prominent physician and activist and son of William Blaisdell, who had served on the jury of the Ala Moana assault trial; and members of the Napoleon family, a well-known and multigenerational family of watermen related to Walter Napoleon, who had served on the jury of the Massie-Fortescue trial. As we left that evening, organizer Craig Howes told the audience that our panel was held on January 8—the very same day that a young Joseph Kahahawai was kidnapped from the front steps of the building in 1932.

In 2004 Carroll's play ran for a few weeks. Stannard's book and the WGBH documentary had not been fully completed yet. And then, in the spring of 2005, Mark Zwonitzer's documentary aired. As Stannard noted in his book, the official release date for his book and for the documentary were, coincidentally, the same day. During half of 2003 and throughout 2004, Zwonitzer and Stannard "spent the better part of the next year openly sharing ideas, information, documents, interviews and photographs—becoming friends in the process." Stannard has said that rather than a competition, the process of sharing information was "one of the most fruitful collaborations" he had ever enjoyed. "We were even able to arrange things so that the publication of the book and the initial airing of the film—*The Massie Affair*—occurred on the same day."[77] Stannard's book generated interest locally and on the continental United States. *Honolulu Magazine* featured a cover story titled "The Crime That Changed the Islands: A New Look at the Massie Case," by Lavonne Leong. *Honor Killing* was also reviewed in San Francisco and New York newspapers. Given the publicity that Stannard's book and Zwonitzer's documentary generated in 2005, Mutual Publishing issued another reprint of *Rape in Paradise* that same year.

In 2006 I moved back to Honolulu to take a job teaching history at Kamehameha Schools in Kapālama. It was there that I met relatives of Joseph Kahahawai and Ben Ahakuelo, two of the principals in the case.[78] Though I was surprised at first to meet these relatives, as I readjusted to living in Honolulu I realized that, after all, I was teaching in the Pālama area of Honolulu—the same neighborhood that had been home to the Kauluwela Boys.

Geography also mattered in many ways. For me, I had to reorient myself, learning again the neighborhoods on Oʻahu where I grew up, went to school, and played. I went to school in Kapālama, and I waited for the city bus after school on School Street at a bus stop just across the street from Puea Cemetery, where Joseph Kahahawai is buried. Little did I know then, in the 1980s, that I would be writing two decades later about Kahahawai and this very area. Puea Cemetery is on the *mauka* side of School Street, just east of the Kamehameha Schools bus terminal, where students wait for rides up the hill to campus. On the other side of the cemetery is the United Public Workers building, which, in some ways, underscores the working-class character of the neighborhood. Kahahawai's well-tended grave is not far from the building. Family and community members place flowers at the site on a regular basis. Well-known island photographers and educators like Kapulani Landgraf and Jan Becket have taken black-and-white photos of the gravesite in order to perpetuate the memory of Joseph Kahahawai.[79] Both are familiar with the Kapālama area, Landgraf being a Kamehameha Schools alumna and Becket a Kamehameha Schools teacher.

When I moved to the University of Hawaiʻi at Mānoa in 2008 to take a newly created position on the history of modern Hawaiʻi in the Department of History, I thought deeply about how I would research, write, and teach about the history of Hawaiʻi. I knew to use my academic training as a historian, but I also felt compelled to bring more interdisciplinary and community-based approaches to the position. I teach my students to evaluate a variety of sources and types of history; I encourage them to look at issues of affect or emotion. Written sources like books, articles, and printed primary sources are important, but so are people. I remind them to value people more than books.

Being at the university, I was also able to interact with other people on a regular basis. For example, I could talk to colleagues in American studies, ethnic studies, and at the Department of English. I spent time at Mānoa Gardens with social scientists from political science, anthropology, and sociology. All along we talked about what it means to live and work in Hawai'i. There is a sense of responsibility that scholars must attend to if they are to work in Hawai'i.

My job-related move from Kamehameha Schools to the university also included a physical move in residence for me and my young family, from Kapālama to Mānoa. When I taught at Kamehameha, we lived just above Puea Cemetery, and now, interestingly enough, we live not too far from the houses that the Massies and Grace Fortescue rented in Mānoa Valley in the early 1930s.

TEACHING ABOUT THE
MASSIE-KAHAHAWAI CASE

Teaching since 2006 in Hawai'i at the high school and college levels has allowed me to better see how the Massie-Kahahawai case has been presented to these students in the last several years. Stannard's book and Zwonitzer's documentary have had the widest impact; field trips to the Judiciary History Center in Honolulu and to other places related to the case have also left a strong impression on students, based on what other instructors have told me. Historian Roy Rosenswieg has noted in *The Presence of the Past* that family and community histories and public history displays at museums, for example, are much more likely to have a lasting impact on students than depictions of events in books alone.

The Massie-Kahahawai case is now mentioned consistently in university courses, mainly in the University of Hawai'i system and trickling down into high school history of Hawai'i courses through teachers who have earned their degrees from the university. I mention the case in my own history of Hawai'i courses, but the effect may be greater when I taught (and continue to teach) about the case as a guest speaker in courses like team-taught humanities and social sciences seminars for future high school teachers. Public school teachers employed by the State of Hawai'i's Department of Education are also likely to come across the case when they complete at least one college course on the history of Hawai'i, which is required for their teaching credentials.[80] High school students most commonly learn about the case in a history of modern Hawai'i class taken in eleventh or twelfth grade. This one-semester, half-credit course is mandatory in order to graduate from public high schools in Hawai'i.[81] Students also sometimes hear about the case in a U.S. history or American government class, or even in a specialized forensic science class like one offered at Farrington High School in Kalihi.

University of Hawai'i courses from the departments of American studies, anthropology, ethnic studies, Hawaiian language, Hawaiian studies, history, and political science, as well as in the Richardson School of Law, discuss the case, often by assigning Stannard's book, using Zwonitzer's documentary, or inviting a guest speaker. Today there is far more extensive discussion about the case than there was thirty to forty years ago, when only ethnic studies courses covered it. In the mid-1990s Professor Marion Kelly told me about how the Massie case has been mentioned in classes since the founding of the program (now a department) in the early 1970s. She even gave me an original copy of John Reinecke's pamphlet from the early 1950s, *The Navy and the Massie-Kahahawai Case,* which she has used at times in her classes.

On the continental U.S., university courses have also discussed the Massie case, sometimes as part of an American studies or ethnic studies class, but most frequently in Asian Pacific American studies classes, which tend to discuss the history of Hawai'i more thoroughly. Again, many university instructors have come across the case through reading Stannard's *Honor Killing* or seeing the *Massie Affair* documentary. The increasing efficiency of resources available online has also facilitated further teaching, research, and discussion about the case.[82]

I have shared my understanding of the Massie case at seminars that train university, community college, and high school teachers from across the continental U.S.—mainly at workshops held at the East-West Center. I was usually asked to discuss military and civilian relations in Hawai'i shortly before and during World War II.[83] Now, teachers can follow up and use Stannard's book and Zwonitzer's documentary, or Internet materials like the WGBH Boston Web page.

It is local, face-to-face interactions, however, that have a greater impact than information on the Massie case found on the Internet. Since the early

1930s the Massie case narrative has been used by locals to negotiate tensions between the grand historical narrative of the continental United States and their lived experiences in Hawaiʻi. Far from being a story buried in the archives, it is one that lives on in popular culture and public discourse. As a story of resistance, it also has the potential to reach other groups and individuals with similar stories to tell.

EPILOGUE

Ha'ina 'ia mai

Ha'ina 'ia mai ana ka puana . . .
Let the story be told . . .

At the closing of many Hawaiian songs, one will often hear the familiar phrase above, signaling to the audience that the song—the story—is coming to an end. Even though they might not be fluent in 'Ōlelo Hawai'i, or the Hawaiian language, most locals today have heard the phrase near the closing of songs often enough to understand that the story is coming to a conclusion. Now that the effects of Hawaiian-language immersion schools and the Hawaiian Renaissance are increasingly felt today, growing numbers of Hawaiian-language speakers, young and old, recognize that "*Ha'ina 'ia mai ana ka puana*" is more accurately an imperative or a command informing listeners that they have a duty *to tell the summary refrain of the story.* The phrase does not signify a conclusion, but instead calls for listeners to return to the beginning, to tell the story again, to perpetuate not only its contents, but also its cadences and manner of telling. It is the repetition of phrases, after all, that reinforces the story, enhances its meaning, and engenders memory, thereby linking the storyteller to other members of the community.

Not all people in Hawai'i today recall the Massie-Kahahawai case. Since most current Hawai'i residents were born after World War II, it might also be difficult for some to imagine a past in which people of Native Hawaiian and Asian ancestry were considered second-class citizens by those on the continent. The Massie case helps to explain the origins of local identity in Hawai'i, but other factors also contributed to its development in the late twentieth century. Though not all locals can claim to be Native Hawaiian, what usually links locals together is their collective belief that they are legitimately connected to Hawai'i and its history in a special way.[1] Since the late 1960s and early 1970s a revival of Native Hawaiian cultural traditions has encouraged locals of varying ethnic backgrounds to position themselves within the narrative of Hawai'i's past through cultural practices unique to the islands. Ethnic studies and community celebrations have also prompted successive generations of locals to look back on Hawai'i's plantation past with a sense of reverence and even nostalgia. This study has shown why the story of the Massie case has been one of the most powerful ways to express local identity—one that is often shared by indigenous Native Hawaiians and the descendants of Asian, Portuguese, and Puerto Rican immigrants who came to Hawai'i to work the fields. Popular narratives of the case appeal to locals because they reach out to ethnic groups and individuals who recognize a common history of racism and oppression.

STRUCTURES OF FEELING:
EMOTIVE ELEMENTS OF
"LOCAL IDENTITY"

Examining the relationship between local experiences and a national history is necessary for any comprehension of local identity in Hawai'i. A large part of the construction of local identity relies on the passing on of unofficial knowledge—knowledge about the past that has often been left out of history books for quite some time. Including the voices of working-class men and women and using oral histories is now commonplace in social histories. This book has gone a step further by suggesting that local identity in Hawai'i has a constitutive emotive element about it that often escapes written accounts. This is not to say that other social phenomena do not have such emotive elements. I am not arguing that Hawai'i is a "special" place, unlike any other—such an approach is too much like the sort of myth making used in selling Hawai'i to tourists seeking the "Paradise of the Pacific" where the

"Aloha Spirit" prevails. In a setting where people seldom move away from the island chain or their particular island, one finds that locals also often reside in the very same neighborhoods in which their parents, grandparents, and even great-grandparents lived. Such a sense of community tends to foster bonds to place and history that are increasingly uncommon in other parts of the United States, particularly the American West, that see high rates of mobility.

Local identity emerged because of the multiple ways that life in Hawai'i was seen—and continues to be seen—as different from life in the continental United States. I have tried to convey the sense of hurt and injustice caused by the Massie-Kahahawai case in Hawai'i. Structural changes in the political economy enabled the formation of local identity in urban Honolulu of the 1930s, but at its deepest level local consciousness formed in the early part of the twentieth century and has since survived because of its strong *emotive* elements. The ties that third-, fourth-, and fifth-generation descendants of immigrants have to their plantation roots are intangible memories that escape quantification. Similarly, the pain that many Native Hawaiians feel more than a century after the overthrow of Queen Lili'uokalani is also an immeasurable, but significant, reminder that events from the past live on in the minds, bodies, and memories of present individuals. Thus large parts of this book show how individuals have continually expressed how they *feel* that Hawai'i is different. As Darlene Clark Hine, a scholar of African American history, and other social historians have noted, even the best social histories often can never tell us how it felt to be a member of an oppressed group in the past.[2] The late Native Hawaiian musician Israel Kamakawiwo'ole, in singing "Hawai'i '78," drew a connection to the Hawaiian monarchy of the past, asking what people then would say about the present condition—not only of Native Hawaiians, but of Hawai'i and its people in general: "How would they feel? Would their smiles be content or would they cry?"

A sociologist from the continent, Avery Gordon, reminds us that emerging scholarship should, too, attempt to capture some of the feeling of human history. Often our histories and our sociological imagination as manufactured by academia move us away from human understandings of the past. We must, as Gordon puts it, examine "haunting": "In haunting, organized forces and systemic structures that appear removed from us make their impact felt in everyday life in a way that confounds our analytic separations and confounds the social separations themselves." We must thus work hard to examine the disjuncture between "identifying a social structure" and its "articulation in everyday life and thought."[3] Kamakawiwoʻole expresses it more succinctly, calling upon listeners to let loose their emotion in order to achieve a more empathetic understanding of the islands' past: "Cry for the gods, cry for the people, cry for the land that was taken away. And then yet, you'll find Hawaiʻi."[4]

"TALKING STORY" AS LOCAL CULTURAL PRACTICE

The Massie case narrative is part of a larger repertoire of stories, songs, dances, foodways, jokes, and other cultural practices that locals use to distinguish themselves from residents on the continental United States. The way in which it has been told and retold through a practice known as "talk story" is familiar to many. To "talk story" is to take part in a communal practice of sharing stories that link past to present. The term is a Hawaiʻi Creole English expression that "characterizes a widespread and social form of oral, animated exchange."[5] According to Stephen Sumida, a literary scholar at the University of Washington and one of the organizers of the Talk Story conferences of 1978 and 1979, "talk story" is comparable to "shooting the breeze" or "chewing the fat," but "'talk story' is Hawaii's own [term], this verbal style being neither quaint nor 'waste time.'"[6] In the 1978 Talk Story conference, Sumida and other literary scholars from Hawaiʻi and the continent found that "[the words] 'talk story' also characterize much of Hawaii's contemporary literature: anecdotes, vignettes, sketches, short fiction, both lyrical and narrative poetry, monodramas filled with the central characters; reminiscences directly addressed to the audience, and entire novels told by a speaker whose genuine voice sounds like someone talking story."[7]

Even among locals themselves, it is as customary to make light of "talk story" as it is to make light of local culture in general. Locals know that as the descendants of native and immigrant peoples of Hawaiʻi, they have come to develop shared gift-giving practices, local food delicacies, and modes of oral communication that, at least from the viewpoint of "Mainlanders," seem to be obtuse and nonconfrontational. It is important that we not trivialize these cultural practices. Even in the early twenty-first century, when print and visual culture tend to predominate, sociologists, anthropologists, and folklorists remind us that storytelling practices among modern people still exist, even among urban dwellers in places like Honolulu.

In 1983, when historian Ronald Takaki opened the preface to his book *Pau Hana: Plantation Life and Labor in Hawaii* by mentioning his "talk story" sessions with his uncle, he pioneered the way for other scholars born or raised in Hawai'i to express their personal links to a history of plantation life that was endured by their families, that was part of a larger experience of Asians living in the United States, and that was part of a greater American history. Takaki's works are lively, readable, and popular because they enable readers to see the connections between individuals' stories, family history, ethnic history, and the dominant American history narrative. In *Pau Hana*, Takaki mentions that he first got the idea to write the book after "talking story" with his Uncle Richard Okawa at his home in Mō'ili'ili. His uncle, realizing that his nephew had written a few books on the history of African Americans and Native Americans on the continent, asked, "Hey, why you no go write a book about us?" Thinking back to how his grandfather had come to the islands as a contract laborer in 1886 and how his mother had been born on a plantation on the Big Island of Hawai'i, Takaki began to understand his uncle's insistence that surely his family's story was one "worthy of serious scholarly attention."[8]

Takaki's uncle's remarks point to the general need for working-class people to have their stories told and recorded in written and "official" form for future audiences and those beyond their particular shores. *Pau Hana* shows the interplay between works of nonfiction and fiction in creating knowledge about Hawai'i. In addition to poring over boxes of documents from the files of the Hawaiian Sugar Planters' Association and bringing life to planters' alphabetized requests for "Fertilizer" and "Filipinos," for example, Takaki quotes novelist Milton Murayama's *All I Asking For Is My Body* (1975) in order to characterize the harsh conditions of Hawai'i plantation life.[9] A decade after Takaki's book appeared, Kayo Hatta's film, *Picture Bride* (1994)—a work of historical fiction—paid homage to *Pau Hana* by paraphrasing a page in which Takaki described the lack of understanding between a planta-tion field boss and his Chinese workers. In the Hatta film, the workers are a multicultural group of Filipino and Japanese laborers, thus also showing the interchangeability of these worker's experiences as "locals" whose class affili-ation as plantation workers transcended their ethnicity. When the men in the fields are unable to comprehend their new *luna* (boss), who speaks standard English, a bystander must translate his instructions into a form of Hawai'i Creole English: "*Luna*, big boss speak, all men down below cutch; suppose too much *mauka* [uphill, high] cutch, too mucha sugar *poho* [wasted]—*keiki* [shoots] no use. Saavy?" Filipino and Japanese workers then laugh at their boss' inability to communicate effectively. In Takaki's *Pau Hana,* a worker replies, "Huy! wasamalla dis *Haole*—he no can taok *haole!*"[10] The scene serves as a reminder of the misunderstanding between those traditionally seen as subordinate and those who like to think that they are in control. Taking a cue from this scene, we must seek not only to listen carefully, but also to retell the past in understandable ways.

Stories about the Massie case in the 1980s and 1990s are distinctive from earlier ones in that they, too, often confuse fact and fiction. That these memories are sometimes "tainted" by details from *Blood and Orchids,* however, does not take away from the fact that they also contribute to and maintain local identity today. *Blood and Orchids* and *Picture Bride,* for that matter, are examples of how popular culture can give increased visibility to a story or a history for a larger, national audience. At the same time, these mediated forms do not necessarily dilute local understandings of such events and histories. If anything, they serve to pique curiosity as to what the "authentic" or "local official" story might be. When *Blood and Orchids* was first broadcast in 1986, locals were acutely aware that the "real" story did not end with a naval officer serving a ten-year sentence at an Oʻahu prison. But in other ways locals could celebrate the fact that the unfair treatment of the people of Hawaiʻi could be told again, this time in a television miniseries that employed local actors with frequent speaking parts alongside famous actors from the continent. Though locals were not 100 percent successful in negotiating the production of *Blood and Orchids,* they always had their own interpretations of the events as they had had throughout every decade since 1931. By the 1980s they also had a measure of political, social, and cultural power greater than during the 1930s as a territory of the United States.

This book did not start out as an exercise in talking story, but for many reasons parts of it approximate this local cultural practice. In large part, the character and the cadences of the oral histories and oral testimony I used in completing this work were reproduced in my own prose. Words recorded over a half-century ago by Richardson and Pinkerton investigators and words of my interviewees in the late twentieth- and early twenty-first centuries came from locals, telling their stories, at their own pace, and often in variants of Hawaiʻi Creole English. The fact that I, too, grew up in Hawaiʻi has also had a considerable effect on the scope, nature, and writing of this book.

In part, this combination of oral and written sources was completed with confidence because I had seen its success before. In James Goodman's *Stories of Scottsboro* (1994) and Theodore Rosengarten's *All God's Dangers* (1975)—two works on African American experiences in the American South completed almost two decades apart—both historians skillfully acknowledged their subject position as authors and how their participation in collecting oral and written accounts profoundly strengthened their histories by adding a more human character to them. I have incorporated the voices of many Hawai'i locals because, like Goodman and Rosengarten, I recognize that they make for engaging social histories, highlighting the day-to-day practices of individuals who might otherwise have been overlooked. Rather than only "giving voice" to these historical agents, I believe I have opened up spaces in the academic realm through which their voices might rightfully be heard. During the Hawaiian Renaissance, writers like George Kanahele and John Dominis Holt recognized that Native Hawaiian voices have always been around despite earlier missionary efforts to limit use of the Hawaiian language. Similarly, local voices have been around for more than eight decades since the Massie-Kahahawai case—it is just that we did not listen closely enough. Taking up a challenge offered at the 1978 Talk Story conference, I present my book as part of a "river of words and books" that are needed if locals are "to turn the tide of silence and misappropriation of Hawaii's cultures."[11] It is offered not as a definitive account, but as a local story of the culture of history in Hawai'i.

CHRONOLOGY OF THE
MASSIE-KAHAHAWAI CASE
AND ITS LEGACY

1931

September 12—Saturday night dance held at the Ala Moana Amusement Park. Naval party at the Ala Wai Inn.

September 13, 12:35 a.m.—Car accident at corner of King and Liliha Streets.

    1:00 a.m.—Mrs. Thalia Massie hails a car, asking the occupants, "Are you white people?"

September 14—Honolulu police start questioning possible suspects.

September 15—Ben Ahakuelo, Horace Ida, Henry Chang, David Takai, and Joseph Kahahawai are brought before Mrs. Massie's hospital bed at Queen's Hospital. She identifies them as her assailants. They are charged with sexual assault.

October 13—Grand jury formally indicts the five alleged assailants.

November 4—The five defendants enter a plea of not guilty.

November 16–17—Jury selection: 1 haole, 1 Portuguese, 6 part-Hawaiian, 2 Japanese, and 2 Chinese.

November 18—Trial of *Territory of Hawaii v. Ahakuelo et al.* begins.

November 25—Kahahawai and Takai take the stand and deny the charges against them.

December 3—Case goes to the jury at 8:45 p.m.

December 5—Jury reports to Judge Alva Steadman that it is unable to agree. Steadman sends jury back for further deliberation.

December 6—After ninety-seven hours of deliberation, judge declares a mistrial. Prosecution plans for a retrial.

December 13—Horace Ida is kidnapped by a group of men in downtown Honolulu. He is taken to the Nuʻuanu Pali, where he is severely beaten and almost thrown off the cliff.

December 14—*Hawaii Hochi* is outraged over Ida's beating. Navy men are suspected.

December 18—Ida is unable to identify any of his assailants during a lineup.

1932

January 8, 8:15 a.m.—Thomas Massie, Grace Fortescue, Albert O. Jones (at home setting up and then left behind), and Edward J. Lord show Joseph Kahahawai a fake summons and kidnap him in front of the courthouse where Kahahawai reports daily, according to the terms of his bail.

8:30 a.m.—Kahahawai's cousin, who witnessed the kidnapping, notifies police.

10:30 a.m.—Police spot the Massie's Buick sedan, driven by Grace Fortescue, and order it to pull over. A car chase ensues all the way to the blowhole lookout at Makapuʻu. Police find Joseph Kahahawai's naked body in the back seat.

January 10—Kahahawai's funeral. *Honolulu Star-Bulletin* reports two thousand in attendance.

January 11—U.S. Senate adopts Senate Resolution no. 134 calling for an investigation into the law enforcement of the Territory of Hawaiʻi. U.S. Attorney General William Mitchell appoints Assistant Attorney General Seth Richardson to head a ten-member team to conduct interviews in Honolulu.

February 4—Seth Richardson and his team arrive in Honolulu to start investigation.

March 24—Clarence Darrow arrives.

March 30—Richardson Report submitted to U.S. Attorney General William Mitchell, who transmits report to Senate on April 4.

April 4—Jury selection begins and is completed on April 7.

April 11—Trial starts.

April 27—Jury sent to deliberate at 5:00 p.m.

April 29—At 5:30 p.m. jury returns a verdict of manslaughter with recommendation for leniency.

May 4—Judge Charles Davis sentences Fortescue, Massie, Lord, and Jones to ten years. Minutes later the Massie-Fortescue group is brought to ʻIolani Palace to see Governor Judd, who commutes their sentences.

May 6 or 7—two to three days after commutation, Lord and Jones leave quietly.

Despite conviction of a crime, the navy does not pursue disciplinary action.

May 8—Four days after commutation, Thalia Massie, Thomas Massie, and Grace Fortescue leave on the SS *Malolo*.

June 15—August 31—Pinkerton Detective Agency investigates the Ala Moana assault, interviewing people in Honolulu, Los Angeles, and New York.

October—Pinkerton Report delivered to Governor Judd. Concludes there is no major evidence to show that Ahakuelo, Ida, Takai, Chang, and Kahahawai committed assault on Thalia Massie.

December 5—Final version of Pinkerton Report submitted to Governor Judd.

1933

February 13—Prosecutor John Kelley makes a motion for *nolle prosequi*, or "no prosecution," in the matter of *Territory of Hawaii v. Ahakuelo, Ida, Chang, and Takai*.

1934

January—Thalia Massie travels to Reno, Nevada, to divorce Thomas Massie. Divorce is granted on February 22 on grounds of "extreme cruelty."

March—Thalia Massie attempts suicide on a cruise ship to Europe. San Francisco maritime strike brings early International Longshoremen's and Warehousemen's Union (ILWU) organizers to the islands.

1937

Three thousand Filipino workers of the Vibora Luviminda participate in the last ethnic-based union strike in Hawai'i.

1938

Fifty-one workers are injured during the "Hilo Massacre."

1941–1944

Territory of Hawai'i under martial law after Japanese war planes bomb Pearl Harbor on December 7, 1941. U.S. District Court declares martial law illegal on June 30, 1944.

1946

ILWU leads twenty-eight thousand workers in the successful, multiethnic 1946
    Sugar Strike.

1951

Majors-Palakiko case prompts the *Honolulu Record* to issue a pamphlet on the
    Massie case authored anonymously by John Reinecke.

1954

Democratic Party wins major victories in territorial elections, undermining the
    Big Five–Republican Party coalition. Democrats win over two-thirds of
    territorial House seats and almost as many in the territorial Senate.

1959

Hawai'i is admitted to the Union as the fiftieth state.
Daniel Inouye represents Hawai'i as the first U.S. congressman of Japanese ancestry.

1961

Thalia Massie, now a student at the University of Arizona, meets a fellow student,
    twenty-one years her junior, and marries him. The marriage lasts only two
    years.

1962

Thalia Massie dies in West Palm Beach, Florida, of an overdose of barbiturates on
    July 2.[1]

1966

Theon Wright publishes *Rape in Paradise*. Peter Van Slingerland publishes *Some-
    thing Terrible Has Happened*. Robert Packer and Bob Thomas publish *The
    Massie Case*.

1967

Former governor Judd tells the *Honolulu Star-Bulletin* that he "acted under the heaviest pressure" in commuting the Massie-Fortescue group's sentences.

1968

Ben Ahakuelo becomes the first and only of the five suspects to grant a newspaper interview.

1970

Ahakuelo dies.

1974

George Ariyoshi, the son of Japanese immigrants, becomes the first non-Caucasian governor of Hawai'i and the first governor of Asian ancestry in the United States.

1983

Norman Katov publishes *Blood and Orchids*.
Lawyer of reputed underworld leader Henry Huihui claims his case has received more publicity than the Massie case.

1986

Television miniseries *Blood and Orchids* airs on CBS.
Governor John Waihee, a Native Hawaiian, is elected governor.

1988–1996

Glen Grant offers monthly tours focusing on the Massie case.

1993

More than twenty thousand mark the centennial of the overthrow of Queen Lili'uokalani in 'Onipa'a observances at 'Iolani Palace.

1994

Benjamin Cayetano elected as the first Filipino American governor in the nation.

1996

Max Allan Collins publishes *Damned in Paradise*.

1997–1998

Hearst-owned Lifetime Channel rebroadcasts *Blood and Orchids*.

2001

University of Hawai'i American studies professor David E. Stannard issues a call for
stories about the Massie-Kahahawai case through the *Honolulu Advertiser*.

2002

Cobey Black's book, *Hawaii Scandal*, is published.

2004

Dennis Carroll's play, *Massie/Kahahawai*, runs at Kumu Kahua Theatre.

2005

David Stannard's book, *Honor Killing*, and Mark Zwonitzer's American Experience
documentary, *The Massie Affair*, are released in April.

2009

"*Hoomanao* (Remember): The Massie Case and Injustice Then and Now" panel
sponsored by the Japanese American Citizens' League and the Japanese
Cultural Center of Hawai'i.
Alan Brennert's novel, *Honolulu*, and Yunte Huang's *Charlie Chan: The Untold Story
of the Honorable Detective and His Rendezvous with American History* featuring details from the Massie case are published.

2010

Poet Gizelle Gajelonia publishes a poem about the Massie case in her chapbook, *Thirteen Ways of Looking at TheBus* (Honolulu: Tinfish Press).

2011

Two trade paperbacks—Bill James' *Popular Crime* (New York: Scribner) and John Farrow's biography, *Clarence Darrow: Attorney for the Damned* (New York: Random House)—are published with extensive discussions about the Massie case.

Four Bamboo Ridge poets—Ann Inoshita, Juliet Lee Kono, Christy Passion, and Jean Toyama—start a collaborative project in writing a *renshi* (linked poem) that runs from August 2011 to May 2012.

NOTES

CHAPTER 1: LOCAL BOYS

1. Papers of Governor Lawrence McCully Judd, HSA, Ala Moana Assault—January 1932 file, "Conversation between D. W. Watson and Ben Ahakuelo at the Honolulu Police Station, Wednesday, January 20, 1932, 2:10–3:15 p.m.," 2.
2. Words of Postmaster Charles F. Chillingworth, according to Pinkerton operative "E. V." Pinkerton Report, HSA: entry for Honolulu, August 1, 1932.
3. Van Slingerland, *Something Terrible Has Happened*; Wright, *Rape in Paradise*; Packer and Thomas, *The Massie Case*.
4. Adams, "Education and Economic Outlook for the Boys of Hawaii, 3–22.
5. Adams, Annual Report of the [Honolulu] Police Department, 3.
6. Ibid., 3–7.
7. Emidio Cabico, "Lucky I Never Work Field," ESOHP interview in *Hanahana*, ed. Kodama-Nishimoto, Nishimoto, and Oshiro, 124.
8. In secondary source texts, Asian American studies scholars have sometimes referred to these strikes in Hawai'i as examples of pan-Asian alliances before World War II. Research into the strikes themselves, however, suggests that most strike activity by Filipino and Japanese laborers was concurrent rather than coordinated. I thank Jonathan Okamura for this repeated observation.
9. Takaki, *Pau Hana*, 65–66.
10. Okamura, "*Aloha Kanaka Me Ke Aloha 'Aina*," 122.
11. Ibid.

12. Ibid., 123.
13. "Pidgin" is the colloquial term used for what linguists call Hawai'i Creole English, or HCE. In recent years some linguists have used the term Hawai'i Creole, noting that English is not necessarily the only basis for grammatical structures in the language. Hawaiian and Portuguese, for example, have a significant impact on Hawai'i Creole. See Sakoda and Siegel, *Pidgin Grammar.*
14. The remarks of one sugar planter cited in Takaki, *Pau Hana,* 65.
15. Reinecke, *Language and Dialect in Hawaii,* 193. Reinecke provides a detailed description of pidgin, or HCE, in this work—a revision of his 1935 master's thesis completed at the University of Hawai'i.
16. Ibid., 193–195.
17. Wright, *Rape in Paradise,* 29.
18. Upon his retirement from the Honolulu Fire Department, Ben Ahakuelo granted Drew McKillips an interview to discuss the Massie case and his son's problems with the law. See "Isles' Most Notorious Case Began in 1931," *Honolulu Advertiser,* June 14, 1968, A3; and Drew McKillips, "'I've Had to Live with This Thing for 35 Years,'" *Honolulu Advertiser,* June 14, 1968, A1.
19. Chang, "Lessons of Tolerance," 115.
20. Undated report of Mrs. Tyssowski, Pinkerton Report interview files.
21. Ibid.
22. For similar recreational activities among Mexican American youths in Los Angeles, see Sánchez, *Becoming Mexican American,* 171–185.
23. For example, see Tamura, *Americanization, Acculturation, and Ethnic Identity.*
24. Some accounts incorrectly state that Ben Ahakuelo made a trip to New York in 1932, but in 1968 Ahakuelo told reporter Drew McKillips that he did not represent the territory in 1932 due to the hysteria generated by the case. McKillips, "'I've Had to Live with This Thing for 35 Years,'" A3.
25. Judd papers, *Terr. of Hawaii vs. Arthur Carter, et al.* file, June 1933. Morimoto, "The Barefoot Leagues."
26. Undated report of Mrs. Tyssowski, Pinkerton Report interview files.
27. Wright, *Rape in Paradise,* 22.
28. With its deep harbors and history of being the center of both royal and territorial governments, O'ahu would come to hold a majority of the archipelago's residents by the early 1920s. The effects of and commentary on the Massie case reached the eight major islands but primarily affected the island of O'ahu.
29. Lind, "Some Ecological Patterns of Community Disorganization in Honolulu," 206.
30. Ibid., 206–207. Lind completed this article a few months prior to the Massie case. The reference to "sex offenses" is to ones cited by Nelligan in his Ph.D. dissertation, "Social Change and Rape Law in Hawaii."
31. Kame'eleihiwa, *Native Land and Foreign Desires,* 3–12.
32. Lind, "Some Ecological Patterns of Community Disorganization in Honolulu," 211–212.
33. Mauricio Mazón argues similarly that Mexican American youths in the famous

"Zoot-Suit Riots" also congregated in gangs of this type. Mazón, *The Zoot-Suit Riots*, 72.

34. Peter Martin, ESOHP participant in *Kalihi, Place of Transition*, 312. Martin is a Portuguese Hawaiian born in Kalihi in 1905; he held various jobs as a lighthouse boat worker, streetcar and trolley conductor, and Pearl Harbor shipyard worker. He played neighborhood sports in the 1920s, playing against Ben Ahakuelo. *Pau* is a Hawaiian word meaning "done" or "finished."

35. Ibid., 315.

36. Ibid.

37. Ibid., 301. During the 1931 rape trial Thalia Massie tried to identify one of her at-tackers, saying that he called for his friend, "Bull." She did not know that the term "bull" was (and still is) commonly used by local males to refer to one another.

38. For more on the distinction between "place" and "space," see Franklin and Steiner, "Taking Place," 3–4. In the same collection, see Yi-Fu Tuan, "Place and Culture," 27–52.

39. Michel de Certeau makes a similar distinction: place "implies an indication of sta-bility" while space involves considerations of "vectors of direction, velocities, and time variables." De Certeau, *The Practice of Everyday Life*, 117.

40. The Portuguese in Hawai'i, imported for work on sugar plantations, were long considered members of the working class and hence not white. By World War II increasing numbers of Portuguese clamored to be considered "white," but because they often do not enjoy positions of privilege, they are still not considered as such. See Geschwender, Carroll-Seguin, and Brill, "The Portuguese and Haoles of Hawaii," 515–527.

41. In keeping with the practice of other scholars of Hawai'i, terms like "Portuguese," "Chinese," and so forth are used to designate ethnic affiliation, not citizenship status.

42. For an in-depth analysis of the social geography of Honolulu for this period, see Lind, *Hawaii's People*, 37–61.

43. ESOHP, *Waikiki, 1900–1985*, xx–xxii.

44. Correa was probably like other elected officials of the period and practiced the art of *ho'omalimali*—campaigning for office throughout the year and securing the favor of constituents through flattery. See Lind, "Voting in Hawaii," Exhibit E of *Administration in Hawaii*, 111.

45. Van Slingerland, *Something Terrible Has Happened*, 16.

46. Thalia Massie later tried to identify her assailants by the clothes they were wearing.

47. I have chosen to use the system of reckoning that is common to people on the island of O'ahu since I believe it to be more accurate and commonsensical in nav-igating the geography of an island than the Western designations of north, south, east, and west. *Mauka* indicates toward the mountains (and thus usually the center of the island); *makai* indicates toward the sea. When in Honolulu, *'ewa* indicates toward 'Ewa Beach, in a roughly westerly direction; and Diamond Head or Koko Head indicates toward these landmarks, in a roughly easterly direction.

48. Henry Chang and Ben Ahakuelo have slightly different recollections and believe that they traveled along Kalākaua Avenue all the way to Beretania, then took a left turn. Van Slingerland believes that the territorial prosecutor in the rape case "was particularly anxious to press this point because, only a few months earlier, Kalakaua Avenue had been extended across King Street to make a shortcut to the next street parallel to King, Beretania. Previously, drivers had to make a two-block dog-leg, via Keeaumoku Street, to reach Beretania." Van Slingerland, *Something Terrible Has Happened,* 49.

49. Theon Wright makes much of this car-jumping incident, whereas Van Slingerland does not mention it at all. See Wright, *Rape in Paradise,* 38–39. A scene in Dennis Carroll's 2004 play, *Massie/Kahahawai,* also highlights this exciting jump between two moving cars.

50. In 1929 Ben Ahakuelo and Henry Chang were arrested for the alleged rape of a local young woman. They were cleared of rape charges but found guilty of "assault with intent to ravish" and sentenced to four months in prison. See Stannard, *Honor Killing,* 109–113.

51. Van Slingerland, *Something Terrible Has Happened,* 21.

52. Wright, *Rape in Paradise,* 59–60.

53. Honolulu police files, 1931, quoted in ibid., 60–61; see also Pinkerton Report, 18, 162–163.

54. McKillips, "'I've Had to Live with this Thing for 35 Years,'" A1.

55. George Sánchez makes a similar argument for the way that public officials viewed Mexican American young men in 1940s Los Angeles. *Becoming Mexican American,* 249–251, 253–258.

56. The name "Ala Moana Boys" shows how the accused were linked to the scene of a crime they were never proven to have committed. I use the term "Kauluwela Boys" since it was a name of their own choosing and links the young men to their place of residence and play.

CHAPTER 2: HAOLE WOMAN

1. Thalia Massie's testimony to Police Inspector John McIntosh of the Honolulu Police Department, Sunday morning, approximately 3:00 a.m., September 13, 1931, at the Massie home on 2850 Kahawai Street in Mānoa Valley. Her testimony is recorded in police files as well as in the Pinkerton Report, 18, 162–163. For a more accessible account of her testimony, see Wright, *Rape in Paradise,* 61–63.

2. Rowlandson, as quoted in Brownmiller, *Against Our Will,* 141.

3. Pinkerton Report, 172–173. Also quoted in Wright, *Rape in Paradise,* 145.

4. Brownmiller, *Against Our Will,* 140–141. Brownmiller provides a brief history of the myth of the African American male as rapist in the chapter titled "A Question of Race" (210–255). She also cogently summarizes a well-known truism of twentieth-century U.S. history: "No single event ticks off America's political schizophrenia with greater certainty than the case of a black man accused of raping a white woman" (210).

5. In another sense, Massie's story of rape articulated issues of race and gender together. As Robyn Wiegman and others have pointed out, while it is important to use analytical categories in scholarship, we should also remember that human beings experience life in a variety of categories. See Wiegman, *American Anatomies*.
6. "We Reach Honolulu," *The Chicago Defender*, January 16, 1932.
7. Stirling, *Sea Duty*, 267.
8. Anderson, *Imagined Communities*, 163–164.
9. Brownmiller, *Against Our Will*. See also Cuklanz, *Rape on Trial*, and Searles and Berger, eds., *Rape and Society*.
10. Ruth Frankenburg and other scholars have studied how American and western European colonial expansion often interwove discourses of whiteness and female purity with racism and colonial discourse. See Frankenburg, *White Women, Race Matters*. For a discussion of the status of American women abroad and gendered colonialism, see Cynthia Enloe's essays, "Nationalism and Masculinity" and "Diplomatic Wives," in her *Bananas, Beaches and Bases*, 42–64, 93–123.
11. Two convicts, Daniel Lyman and Lui Kaikapu, escaped Oʻahu Prison on New Year's Eve. The two had perhaps been let out of prison informally in order to procure a supply of ʻōkolehao (homemade liquor) for a New Year's Eve party to be enjoyed by both prisoners and their wardens. The two split up and Kaikapu stole a car. He broke into the Wilhelmina Rise home of Mrs. James Odowda on the morning of January 2 and allegedly beat her, tied her up, and raped her. Van Slingerland, *Something Terrible Has Happened*, 135–136.
12. "The Hysteria Dies," *Jitsugyo-no-Hawaii*, February 1932 (no day given). Clipping found in Victor Houston Papers, file 143, HSA.
13. Ibid.
14. Du Puy, *Hawaii and Its Race Problem*, 96.
15. The 1930 U.S. Census classified 46,114 territory residents as "Spanish" or "Other Caucasian"; 40,238 of these white residents lived in Honolulu County. Although the census classified Portuguese and Puerto Ricans as "Caucasian," these groups were historically plantation laborers and thus not considered part of the haole power elite. Based on data from "Table 19.—Composition of the Population, For Counties and For Hilo and Honolulu: 1930," *Fifteenth Census of the United States*, 68.
16. Eleanor Heavey, "Mind, Body and Soul," in Kodama-Nishimoto, Nishimoto, and Oshiro, eds., *Hanahana*, 33.
17. Social historian and folklorist Américo Paredes has pointed to the need to understand the range of terms that groups in the United States have used for one another. Paredes has found that the term "gringo" has long been a derogatory term among Spanish-speaking people for non–Spanish-speaking foreigners. See Paredes, *Folklore and Culture on the Texas-Mexican Border*, 34. The Native Hawaiian term "haole" is similar in that it is thought to refer originally to all non–Hawaiian-speaking foreigners, regardless of skin color or ethnic background.
18. Historian David E. Stannard believes that haole is not inherently a derogatory term. He notes that "*haole* is a widely-understood Hawaiian word that even 19th

century missionaries used in referring to themselves, and it seems both appropriate and preferable, when in Hawai'i and writing about Hawaiian history, to use Hawaiian phrases when they do not hinder communication with English-only speakers." Stannard, *Before the Horror,* 144n1.

19. For more on the term "haole," see Whittaker, *The Mainland Haole,* 1–45, and Rohrer, *Haoles in Hawai'i.*

20. The terms *malihini* and *kama'āina* do not appear to have been commonly used in Hawaiian- and English-language print media until the early twentieth century. The more general "haole" has been used since the times of Captain Cook.

21. Fuchs, *Hawaii Pono,* 67.

22. David Roediger identifies this point in W. E. B. Du Bois' 1935 classic study, *Black Reconstruction in the United States, 1860–1880.* Roediger, *The Wages of Whiteness,* 12.

23. Lind, *An Island Community,* 16–17.

24. Fuchs, *Hawaii Pono,* 66. According to the 1930 U.S. Census, three quarters of the haole population lived in the urban centers of Honolulu (on O'ahu) and Hilo (on Hawai'i Island). Only 7.7 percent lived in the rural districts of O'ahu. Military personnel are not included in these census figures.

25. Coulter and Serrao, "Manoa Valley, Honolulu," 109. Coulter and Serrao also note that a fair number of Japanese American women acted as live-in maids in some haole households. Some worked as maids in Mānoa but resided in other parts of Honolulu.

26. Undated letter from Grace Fortescue to her mother, late December 1931 or early January 1932, from 2850 Kahawai Street, Honolulu, Hawai'i. This letter was found in the private manuscript file of territorial prosecutor John C. Kelley, HSA. It apparently was given to Kelley by the Massie-Fortescue party in the hopes of helping Kelley prepare for a second trial against the Kauluwela Boys. As a territorial prosecutor Kelley worked on both sides of the Massie case: in fall of 1931 he was the lead prosecutor in the rape trial; in spring of 1932 he was the territorial prosecutor who defeated Clarence Darrow in the murder trial.

27. George Lipsitz has commented on a similar situation in the continental United States since the mid-1960s. Lipsitz, "*Lean on Me:* Beyond Identity Politics," in Lipsitz, *The Possessive Investment in Whiteness,* 139–157.

28. Nelligan, "Social Change and Rape Law in Hawaii."

29. Van Slingerland, *Something Terrible Has Happened,* 181.

30. Fay King, "News of Violence in Beautiful Honolulu Comes as Shock"; syndicated 1932 Daily Mirror, Inc., feature, clipped and sent to Victor Houston, ca. January 1932. This short article is accompanied by a series of three drawings of a hula girl, an ukulele player, and lei-wearing tourists. Victor Houston Papers, file 142, HSA.

31. Hormann, "The Caucasian Minority," *Social Process in Hawaii* 14 (1950): 49; and Lawrence Fuchs, *Hawaii Pono,* 66–67.

32. Dean MacCannell and other scholars of tourism have often noted the relative privilege that tourists and other temporary visitors enjoy at the expense of resident, laboring populations. See MacCannell, *The Tourist.*

33. Thalia and Thomas Massie lived at 2850 Kahawai Street—a place name that many at the time found ironically similar to that of Thalia's alleged assailant, Joseph Kahahawai. Kahahawai later died at the house rented by Grace Fortescue, about a half-mile away on Kolowalu Street. Both houses still stand today.

34. Judith Walkowitz has similarly described how the city of London became a contested terrain by the end of the nineteenth century—one of "dreadful delight," full of "new commercial spaces, new journalistic practices, and a range of public spectacles and reform activities" that inspired "a different set of social actors to assert their own claims to self-creation in the public domain." Waikīkī underwent similar changes in the early twentieth century as tourism and its amusements and small businesses competed with the residential spaces of working-class locals who had resided there for decades. Waikīkī was no London, but it was increasingly compared to seaport towns worldwide with a reputation for excitement and possible danger. Walkowitz, *City of Dreadful Delight,* 18.

35. Wright, *Rape in Paradise,* 19. One of my interviewees counters this assertion. Mānoa resident Miriam Woolsey Reed said that locals also enjoyed the Japanese tea house that Saturday night, and she did not recall large numbers of navy people there. She did not know that the Massies and other navy couples were there until she was questioned on Sunday by Detective John Jardine of the Honolulu Police Department. Reed interview, March 10, 1997.

36. Wright, *Rape in Paradise,* 19.

37. This estimation of the marriage was made by Theon Wright. Peter Van Slingerland's portrayal of the Massies' marriage is similar, and many accounts seem to blame Thalia for having a disagreeable personality. Van Slingerland, for example, described her as "distant, casting a spell of doom whenever she was forced to go to a party." Van Slingerland, *Something Terrible Has Happened,* 12–13. These are gendered descriptions of Thalia's character and demeanor. The wives of naval officers were expected to be pleasant and agreeable.

38. Wright, *Rape in Paradise,* 21. Reed confirms that there were no tables at tea houses like this one. Patrons sat on the floor.

39. Wright, *Rape in Paradise,* 23. Freitas was called to the stand in the Ala Moana assault trial and testified that he saw Thalia Massie arrive at the inn with her head down. Other witnesses made similar observations about the "woman in the green dress" whom they saw that evening.

40. Van Slingerland, *Something Terrible Has Happened,* 4–10.

41. Wright, *Rape in Paradise,* 44.

42. Van Slingerland, *Something Terrible Has Happened,* 22. Wright's account of the phone conversation is, "Please come home. Something awful has happened." Wright, *Rape in Paradise,* 45.

43. Wright, *Rape in Paradise,* 47.

44. See the epigraph at the beginning of this chapter for Thalia Massie's exact words as recorded in the police record.

45. Wright, *Rape in Paradise,* 45–46.

46. Again, it is not my intent to cover the rape and murder trials in great detail, but instead to show how varying interpretations of the trials' outcomes contributed to the formation of local identity in Hawai'i. Wright and Van Slingerland have already provided thorough renderings of the trials. See Wright, "The Ala Moana Trial," 138–167, and "The Massie-Fortescue Trial," 216–236, in *Rape in Paradise*; and Van Slingerland, "The Ala Moana Case," 59–118, and "*The Territory of Hawaii vs. Grace Fortescue, et al.*," 225–302, in *Something Terrible Has Happened*.

47. Van Slingerland's assessment of the mixed jury was seven nonwhites and five whites—the opposite of Theon Wright's assessment. (Van Slingerland, *Something Terrible Has Happened*, 92.) Since Wright was a longtime resident and reporter in Honolulu familiar with its racial classification scheme, I have favored Wright's estimation of the jury. Wright and the *Honolulu Star-Bulletin* listed the names and occupations of the jury for the record. (*Honolulu Star-Bulletin*, November 18, 1931; Wright, *Rape in Paradise*, 140–141.)

48. Wright, *Rape in Paradise*, 138.

49. Pittman was originally from Vicksburg, Mississippi, and moved to Hawai'i in 1915. He was a well-respected lawyer in the islands who later served as attorney general of the territory from 1934 until his death in 1936. Marumoto, "The Ala Moana Case and the Massie-Fortescue Case Revisited," 274n13.

50. Wright, *Rape in Paradise*, 142.

51. Ala Moana assault trial transcript, Judd Papers, HSA.

52. Wright, *Rape in Paradise*, 145–146.

53. League of Women Voters of Hawaii Papers, Private Manuscript File M-356, HSA.

54. Van Slingerland, *Something Terrible Has Happened*, 181.

55. *Honolulu Advertiser*, January 26, 1932. Houston had responded three years before to the calls of the League of Women Voters: "Houston Moves to Get Women on Jury Here," *Honolulu Advertiser*, April 19, 1929. During April 1929 Houston also pushed for immigration measures that would allow Chinese men in Hawai'i to bring over their Chinese wives.

56. This law amended chapter 118 of the *Revised Laws of Hawaii 1925* by adding fourteen new sections calling for a police commission of five members appointed by the governor (as opposed to the old system of a high sheriff). The police commission would then have the power to appoint or remove a police chief who "must at the time of his appointment have been a resident of the Territory for five years." *Laws of the Territory of Hawaii*, 1–7.

57. Act 10, "An Act to Amend Chapter 238 of the *Revised Laws of Hawaii 1925*, Relating to Rape, Abduction and Seduction by Amending Sections 4147 and 4156 Thereof," *Laws of the Territory of Hawaii*, 15–16.

58. Explanation of the territory's law on rape by Judge Alva Steadman in his instructions to the jury of the Ala Moana assault trial. Recorded in Van Slingerland, *Something Terrible Has Happened*, 116.

59. Perhaps we can be certain only of the physical blows and the bullet to Kahahawai's body that resulted in his death. According to the coroner Dr. Faus: "Kahahawai

was shot at the base of the left lung by a .32 caliber steel-jacketed bullet. The bullet entered near the nipple and passed through the lower portion of the lung, lodging in the back, to the right of the spine near the seventh rib, where it was found against the skin and removed. The only other mark on the body was a small abrasion above the left eye which might have been made by a blow. The wristwatch on Kahahawai's arm had stopped at 9:45 [a.m.]. The sheet in which the body was wrapped had been clipped so that no laundry marks were left." Quoted in Van Slingerland, *Something Terrible Has Happened*, 160.

60. "'Sorry, But He Deserved It' Says Ala Moana Case Victim," *Honolulu Advertiser*, January 9, 1932.

61. Territorial prosecutor John Kelley received over 160 letters from people who could not understand how a white man could defend nonwhites accused of raping a white woman. Several sent newspaper clippings with their letters to let Kelley know what "decent people" in their communities thought of him. One man from San Antonio, Texas, for example, quoted radio announcer Floyd Gibbons in asking why Kelley and other white officials in Honolulu were "joining their yellow brothers" instead of defending white women in Hawai'i. (See Letter of J. P. O. to John Kelley, May 11, 1932, Kelley Papers, HSA.)

62. Fuchs, *Hawaii Pono*, 67.

CHAPTER 3: THE KILLING OF JOSEPH KAHAHAWAI

1. Remarks by David Kama as recorded by Theon Wright, *Rape in Paradise*, 198. These remarks are also found in the *Honolulu Record* pamphlet on the Massie case. The *Honolulu Record* states that a groan could be heard among Native Hawaiians in the crowd: "*Hilahila ole keia poe haole!*" ("Shame on these haoles!"); *The Navy and the Massie-Kahahawai Case*, 24.

2. Once again, in keeping with current cultural practices within the State of Hawai'i, the term "Hawaiian" is used in reference only to *Native* Hawaiians throughout this work. Residents of Hawai'i usually do not call themselves "Hawaiian" unless they are indeed Native Hawaiian or part-Native Hawaiian. Current federal legislation defines a Native Hawaiian as "any individual who is a descendant of the aboriginal people who, prior to 1778, occupied and exercised sovereignty in the area that now comprises the State of Hawai'i." Island residents who are not ethnically Hawaiian will sometimes refer to themselves variously as "locals," "longtime residents of Hawai'i," or "*kama'āinas*" in order to express their links to Hawai'i as a special, cultural place. Non-Hawaiian residents rarely refer to themselves as "Hawaiian" in the same way that individuals of varying ethnic backgrounds might adopt an identity linked to their state—e.g., "Californians," "Oregonians," etc.

3. Works in modern European social history have played a role in expanding historians' conceptions of the political. In German history, for example, historians like Detlev Peukert provide a "history of everyday life" during the Weimar and Third Reich years. In his opinion it is crucial—especially in assessing the impact

of modernity in the early twentieth century—to see how day-to-day decisions affected degrees of formal political participation. See Peukert, "The History of Everyday Life," 21–25.

4. Stannard, *Before the Horror.*

5. Sai, *UA MAU KE EA,* 87–95.

6. For more on Hawai'i's political status, see Bell, *A Last among Equals.* The Insular Cases of the early twentieth century also shed more light on the range of options available to the United States in doling out political and civic rights to territories and the inhabitants of recently acquired lands.

7. Hawkins, "Princess Abigail Kawananakoa," 163–177.

8. Based on data from "Table 19.—Composition of the Population, for Counties and For Hilo and Honolulu: 1930," *Fifteenth Census of the United States,* 68. The number of haole elites can be estimated by subtracting the number of Portuguese and Spanish from the "Caucasian" figure for this census year.

9. This cemetery, sometimes overgrown with weeds and the project of community cleanups, still stands along School Street between the United Public Workers' building and the bus terminal for the Kamehameha Schools.

10. "Thousands at Services for Joe Kahahawai," *Star-Bulletin,* January 11, 1932.

11. Ibid. For more on Kumalae, who was also well known as an ukulele maker, see Ruby, ed., *Mō'ili'ili,* 243.

12. "Calm Reigns in City Today as Police Patrol," *Star-Bulletin,* January 11, 1932.

13. Verbal accounts tell of some local Honolulu merchants who briefly moved their curio sales to Hilo during late 1931 and early 1932 so as not to lose their clientele of off-duty sailors. Personal communication, Michiko Kodama, Center for Oral History, University of Hawai'i, July 1996.

14. "Few Brawls in Spite of Wild Rumors," *Advertiser,* December 21, 1931.

15. "Pettengill Is Surprised by Attack on Ida," *Star-Bulletin,* December 14, 1931. Pettengill's name has been spelled "Pettingill" by sources like Reinecke (anonymously), *The Navy and the Massie-Kahahawai Case,* 22, and Chaplin, *Presstime in Paradise,* 181. See also Richard Borreca, "Dark Times Cloud a Land of Sunshine: A 1924 Labor Strike Turns Deadly, and a Sensational 1931 Murder Case Stirs Calls for Military Rule," *Star-Bulletin,* August 9, 1999, http://archives.starbulletin.com/1999/08/09/millennium/story4.html.

16. "Hawaiian Civic Demands Pettengill to Retract Statement On Unsafety," *Nippu Jiji,* December 22, 1931.

17. "No Rioting In Honolulu, Is Navy Report," *Star-Bulletin,* December 14, 1931.

18. The incidence and size of riots are often difficult to confirm, either by oral or written sources. For example, Mauricio Mazón has noted that in World War II Los Angeles, riots between servicemen and Mexican American zoot suiters went on for three days before the *Los Angeles Times* reported them on June 6, 1943. (Mazón, *The Zoot-Suit Riots,* 75.) During the Massie case, aside from a few reports of fights between locals and servicemen reported in Honolulu newspapers, I have not found any sources, oral or written, that suggest violence in December 1931 or January

1932 on the scale of a large riot. Many describe the period as being especially "tense" between locals and nonlocals; some newspapers even took to reporting minor incidents when local young men driving by in cars would yell epithets at white women.

19. Nelligan, "Social Change and Rape Law in Hawaii."
20. "Admiral Pratt Places Himself above Law and Order by His Statement on Death of Kahahawai, the Rev. Leavitt Declares," *Star-Bulletin,* January 11, 1932.
21. Stirling, *Sea Duty,* 253. Stirling probably meant Nuʻuanu Valley.
22. "Thousand at Services for Joe Kahahawai," *Star-Bulletin,* January 11, 1932.
23. Ibid.
24. Several scholars have noted the history and meaning of "Hawaiʻi Ponoʻi"; see Buck, *Paradise Remade,* 118; Charlot, *Hawaiian Poetry of Religion and Politics,* 9–23; and Elbert and Mahoe, eds., *Na Mele O Hawaiʻi Nei,* 43–44.
25. Charlot notes that the song expressed Kalākaua's cultural nationalism and called to mind important themes of his policy: "a unified nation structured in descending ranks; an activist king in the Kamehameha I tradition; a racial emphasis. . . . Also discreet is the religious but non-Christian character of the anthem. All references to the Christian God are omitted." Charlot, *Hawaiian Poetry of Religion and Politics,* 22–23, as quoted in Buck, *Paradise Remade,* 118.
26. Elbert and Mahoe, eds., *Na Mele o Hawaiʻi Nei,* 43–44.
27. Liliʻuokalani might not have thought "Aloha ʻOe" appropriate for Kahahawai's funeral; when the song was sung at the funeral of a missionary friend, the queen is said to have been quite shocked. She composed it as a love song, but it is commonly sung as a general farewell. Elbert and Mahoe, eds., *Na Mele o Hawaiʻi Nei,* 35–36.
28. Kekuni Blaisdell in Mast and Mast, eds., *Autobiography of Protest in Hawaiʻi,* 369. See also Native Hawaiians Study Commission, Report on the Culture, Needs and Concerns of Native Hawaiians.
29. Novelist Norman Katov was quite taken with Abigail Kawananakoa's life story and improvised on it, creating the character of Princess Luahine, who would play a central role in his book, *Blood and Orchids.*
30. For a history of Kamehameha the Great's period of rule, see Daws, *Shoal of Time,* 29–60.
31. Silva, "*Kuʻe!*" 2–15.
32. King Kalākaua designated his sister, Liliʻuokalani (1838-1917), and then Princess Victoria Kaiʻulani (1875-1899) as the first two heirs to the throne. During her reign as monarch, Liliʻuokalani designated Prince David Kawananakoa (1868-1908) and his brother, Prince Kūhiō (1871-1922) as heirs. By the 1930s, there was effectively "no more royalty in Hawaii by blood or by courtesy," in the eyes of many journalists on the continent; Abigail Campbell Kawananakoa (1882-1945) was often called "Princess" because of her marriage to Prince David Kawananakoa.

Periodicals on the continental U.S. followed the actions of Abigail Kawananakoa's playboy son, David Kalākaua Kawananakoa (1904-1953), who was nothing like the nineteenth-century monarch after whom he was named. In 1932, the same year of the Massie case, he recklessly crashed his car at the Pali, killing his passenger, Felicity Conners of California. Five years later, in a drunken rage at his home, he hurled a plate at his girlfriend, and in a freakish accident, a broken shard killed Arwille Kinsella, a part-Hawaiian. Kawananakoa pleaded guilty to manslaughter and was sentenced to ten years. In addition, an older ten-year sentence for the negligent manslaughter of Felicity Conners was reimposed, giving him a total of twenty years. A prison board in 1938 fixed his sentence at five years for good behavior; Kawananakoa was released in July 1941. (*American Weekly,* July 1945.) This story made the family notorious and the subject of much criticism, despite Abigail Kawananakoa's defense of locals and calls for justice during the Massie case.

33. "Women's League Planned to Aid Republicanism," *Star-Bulletin,* November 26, 1928.
34. Buck, *Paradise Remade,* 117–118.
35. Lind, "Voting in Hawaii," in *Administration in Hawaii,* 111.
36. *Star-Bulletin,* July 28, 1932.
37. *Hawaii Hochi,* May 20, 1932.
38. Ibid. Dillingham was on the defensive and now had to write and disseminate his famous "private memorandum" in the hopes of swaying Congress and keeping big business firmly in charge of the Territory of Hawai'i.
39. Based on data from "Table 19.—Composition of the Population, For Counties and For Hilo and Honolulu: 1930," *Fifteenth Census of the United States,* 68. For additional voting statistics for 1930, see Lind, "Voting in Hawaii," *Administration in Hawaii,* 110–112.
40. The term "Oriental vote" was a contemporary one used in Hawai'i social science literature and newspapers of the 1920s and 1930s.
41. Adams, "Exhibit D," in *Administration in Hawaii,* 104–105.
42. Romanzo Adams has noted that the Japanese of the issei, or first generation, were rather firm in instructing their nisei children to marry other Japanese.
43. Judd Papers, HSA, Ala Moana Assault—January 1932 file: Item titled "Conversation between D. W. Watson and Ben Ahakuelo at the Honolulu Police Station, Wednesday, January 20, 1932, 2:10–3:15 p.m.," 2.
44. Letter from Jonah Kūhiō Kalaniana'ole to John Lane, April 6, 1906, as quoted by Fuchs, *Hawaii Pono,* 167.
45. Kawananakoa had advocated for women to be placed on juries as early as 1930. "Princess Says She Aids Women," *Honolulu Star-Bulletin,* October 14, 1930.
46. "Princess Sees Farce in Close of Death Case," *Honolulu Star-Bulletin,* May 4, 1932.
47. David Kama, as recorded by Wright, *Rape in Paradise,* 309.
48. Investigations were unable to link this assault directly to the Massie case. Some locals, however, believed that the Massie case contributed to such anti-Native Hawaiian hostilities. (Pinkerton Report—Report of H. J. B. in Los Angeles, August 9, 1932, HSA.) See also "Kalili Brothers Beaten in Los Angeles Lodgings by Unidentified Intruder," *Honolulu Star-Bulletin,* February 13, 1932.
49. See Ernest Beaglehole's sections on stereotypes of Native Hawaiians in *Some Modern Hawaiians.*

50. Ah Quon McElrath, personal interview, March 14, 1997, Honolulu, Hawai'i. See also Wright, *Rape in Paradise*, 306.

CHAPTER 4: A CLOSING AND AN OPENING

1. Van Slingerland, *Something Terrible Has Happened*, 199.
2. Radiogram from Rear Admiral Stirling to Secretary of the Navy Charles Francis Adams III suggesting change of venue to the District of Columbia, January 26, 1932; Montgomery Winn, lawyer for the Massie-Fortescue group, to Representative Virgil Chapman of Kentucky suggesting D.C. or Kentucky. See Van Slingerland, *Something Terrible Has Happened*, 201.
3. Crim. No. 11891 (1st Cir. Ct. Hawaii 1932).
4. The term "race issue" was one used by contemporary sources at that time; it is similar to the "race card" referred to in the O. J. Simpson case of the 1990s. In the mid-1960s Theon Wright also wrote extensively about how Darrow, in neglecting to familiarize himself with racial conditions in Hawai'i, ultimately fared poorly against territorial prosecutor John Kelley. Wright, *Rape in Paradise*, 218–221.
5. Italics added. This sentence is underlined both in Governor Judd's copy of Judge Cristy's instructions to the jury and in a copy at the Hawaiian Collection of the University of Hawai'i's Hamilton Library by readers who have read these documents over the years. U.S. Congress, Senate, "Charges Against Official Acts of Judge A. M. Cristy, of Hawaii: Letter from Rudolph Bukeley to Senator Kenneth McKellar, of Tennessee."
6. Van Slingerland, *Something Terrible Has Happened*, 227.
7. Wright, *Rape in Paradise*, 202; Reinecke (anonymously), *The Navy and the Massie-Kahahawai Case*, 20; Van Slingerland, *Something Terrible Has Happened*, 216–217.
8. Masaji Marumoto was a young attorney recently admitted to the Hawai'i bar in November 1930. Marumoto worked as an associate in Thompson's Honolulu law office from January 2, 1931, to June 30, 1932. Marumoto, "The Ala Moana Case and the Massie-Fortescue Case Revisited," 271.
9. Kelley was originally from Butte, Montana, but moved to Hawai'i in 1921. Ulrich came from Chicago and settled in Hawai'i in 1925. Marumoto, "The Ala Moana Case and the Massie-Fortescue Case Revisited," 280.
10. Marumoto, in "The Ala Moana Case and the Massie-Fortescue Case Revisited," gives the names of seven of the prominent jurors. The six Caucasian jurors were:
    John Stone, assistant secretary of Castle & Cooke (a Big Five firm); elected as jury foreman
    Theodore Bush, an engineer for Bishop Estate
    Olaf Sorensen, assistant department manager of Oahu Railway & Land Company (owned by Walter Dillingham's family, and the only railroad on the island of O'ahu)
    Charles Strohlin, pump manager of Oahu Sugar Company

Shadford Waterhouse, teller at Bishop National Bank (Hawaiʻiʻs
    oldest bank) and nephew of John Waterhouse, president of
    Alexander and Baldwin (a Big Five Firm)
    Willy Beyer, an independent caterer
  Marumoto identified Theodore Char, a certified public accountant and graduate of the University of Illinois, as one of the Chinese Americans. Wright says that
the other Chinese American was Kam Tai Lee, a cold-storage company employee
and graduate of the University of Hawaiʻi. Wright, *Rape in Paradise*, 220.

11. On Kelley's desk during the trial sat an impressive five boxes of evidence. Van Slin-
    gerland, *Something Terrible Has Happened*, 237.
12. Wright, *Rape in Paradise*, 228, and Van Slingerland, *Something Terrible Has
    Happened*, 131.
13. Darrow as quoted by Van Slingerland, *Something Terrible Has Happened*, 246. See
    also p. 227 of that book.
14. *New York Times* quoted by Van Slingerland, *Something Terrible Has Happened*, 245.
    Circa Friday, ninth day of the trial.
15. Van Slingerland, *Something Terrible Has Happened*, 252, and Wright, *Rape in Para-
    dise*, 235.
16. Testimony of Lieutenant Thomas Massie when questioned by Clarence Darrow,
    also cited by Van Slingerland, *Something Terrible Has Happened*, 252.
17. Wright believes that Massie slipped up in his testimony and almost revealed details
    that he could not have known had he indeed blacked out.
18. Wright, *Rape in Paradise*, 239.
19. Van Slingerland, *Something Terrible Has Happened*, 242.
20. Ibid., 262. Van Slingerland refers to "the supposed abortion."
21. Ibid., 243.
22. Wright, *Rape in Paradise*, 234–235. Judith Walkowitz's work has shown that wom-
    en's reproductive organs are often the objects of medical and scientific inquiries,
    and they can also be presented as "evidence" in legal inquiries, legislative or judicial.
    In examining the use of women's bodies before the law, Walkowitz, Susan Brown-
    miller, Carol Smart, and other scholars have consistently found such legal forums
    to be places where decidedly male biases and patterns of patriarchy dominate. See
    Walkowitz, *Prostitution and Victorian Society* and *City of Dreadful Delight*. See also
    Smart, *Feminism and the Power of Law*, and Brownmiller, *Against Our Will*.
23. Van Slingerland, *Something Terrible Has Happened*, 227.
24. Ibid., 226.
25. Ibid., 244–245; see also the United Press International photos between pp. 118 and
    119 of that book.
26. The sheet (the contents of which were not exactly known to the public and which
    was destroyed by Thalia Massie) was a class questionnaire and could be viewed
    more along the lines of a teacher-student relationship. Nevertheless, three decades
    later Dr. Lowell Kelley, the University of Hawaiʻi psychology professor who had
    administered the questionnaire, went to great lengths to show that he had not

given the sheet of paper to prosecutor John Kelley (no relation). After the late 1960s publication of *Rape in Paradise* and *Something Terrible Has Happened,* Dr. Kelley employed lawyers to clear his name and asserted that it was the Board of Regents of the University of Hawai'i that had removed the document in question from his office and surrendered it to the territorial prosecutor. Judd Papers, HSA.

27. Wright, *Rape in Paradise,* 268. The text of the closing arguments can be found in Larson and Marshall, eds., *The Essential Words and Writings of Clarence Darrow.*
28. Van Slingerland, *Something Terrible Has Happened,* 268.
29. Ibid., 277–280.
30. Ibid., 291.
31. Darrow, *The Story of My Life,* 477.Wright reports that Darrow talked with reporters quite often, commenting to reporters from the islands, "You newspaper fellows down here know the way these people think. How do you figure them out? How do you measure the mentality of Chinese—or part Hawaiians? I can figure out pretty well what the white people are thinking, but I can't tell anything about what these fellows think from their expression, because they don't seem to have any expression." Wright, *Rape in Paradise,* 219.
32. Marumoto, "The Ala Moana Case and the Massie-Fortescue Case Revisited," 283.
33. Van Slingerland, *Something Terrible Has Happened,* 292.
34. Wright, *Rape in Paradise,* 255.
35. Ibid., 219.
36. Ibid., 306.
37. White, *The Content of the Form,* 20.
38. Ibid., 21.
39. *Nippu Jiji,* May 5, 1932.
40. Alessandro Portelli argues that there can be separate judicial truths and historical truths in narratives about courtroom dramas. Portelli, "The Oral Shape of the Law: The 'April 7 Case,'" in *The Death of Luigi Trastulli and Other Stories,* 268.
41. White, *The Content of the Form,* 21.
42. Charles Lindbergh Jr. was kidnapped in New Jersey on March 1, 1932. His body was found months later, on May 12, 1932. The kidnapping trial was held in the winter of 1934–1935.
43. Wright, *Rape in Paradise,* 310.

CHAPTER 5: STORY, MEMORY, HISTORY

1. Malo, *Hawaiian Antiquities,* 1.
2. Bodnar, *Remaking America,* 1.
3. Lipsitz, *Time Passages,* 5.
4. For a discussion of the accepted use of popular memory and collective memory in the historical discipline, see the forum that includes Crane, "Writing the Individual Back into Collective Memory," 1372–1385, and Confino, "Collective Memory and Cultural History," 1386–1403.

5. See, e.g., Okihiro, "Oral History and the Writing of Ethnic History," 27–46.
6. There is a large body of literature, e.g., that addresses memories of the Shoah, or the Holocaust, in modern Europe. In U.S. history circles, some of the earliest social historians of the United States focused their attention on the American South. Many made use of oral interviews of former African American slaves collected during the Depression years under the Works Progress Administration. One of the most celebrated and pioneering of these works centered on the life of one individual: Theodore Rosengarten's biography of Nate Shaw was based on hours of oral history. Rosengarten foregrounded Shaw's voice throughout, allowing Shaw to tell his own history of "his region, class, and race" in Alabama. The story of this black tenant farmer was one of struggle—one not particularly unique for its time and place, but one that was "historically significant *because* it is common" (emphasis added). Rosengarten, *All God's Dangers*, xvi, xxi.
7. Joseph Wong, personal communication, July 10, 1996, Kula, Maui, Hawai'i.
8. Fortescue, "The Honolulu Martyrdom," 5.
9. *Liberty* magazine, like others in Macfadden's publishing empire, was aimed at men and women who sought to improve themselves and their abilities. The six-page article bears a note at the top of the first page, "Reading time: 26 minutes 20 seconds." Fortescue, "The Honolulu Martyrdom," 5–10.
10. Adams, "Hawaiian Horror," 6–13, 80–85. Walter Adams (1892–1942) at one time worked for the *Honolulu Advertiser*. For more on the life of fitness guru and publishing giant Bernarr Macfadden, see Joseph F. Wilkinson, "Look at Me," 136–138, 143–151.
11. Chapin, *Shaping History*, 154.
12. Darrow, "The Massie Trial," 213–218.
13. Yates Stirling Jr., "Honolulu Horror," *True Detective*, February 1939.
14. Stirling, *Sea Duty*, 245.
15. Stannard, *Honor Killing*, 104.
16. HSPA letter dated January 15, 1932, to Governor Judd including four enclosures, Judd Papers, HSA.
17. Dillingham, *A Memorandum*. See also Melendy, *Walter Francis Dillingham*, 218–219.
18. Melendy, *Walter Francis Dillingham*, 182.
19. Anthony, *Hawaii under Army Rule*, x, 39–40.
20. See Pratt, *Hawaii*.
21. Burrows, *Hawaiian Americans*, 115.
22. Ibid., 123.
23. Holmes, *The Specter of Communism in Hawaii*, 186, 142.
24. [Reinecke, anonymously], *The Navy and the Massie-Kahahawai Case*, i.
25. Ibid., 37.
26. Ibid., ii.
27. Ibid., 29.
28. See Chuck Frankel, "Massie Case: All Hawaii's Trial by Jury That Began with a Party Sept. 12, 1931," *Honolulu Star-Bulletin*, September 26, 1966.

29. [Reinecke, anonymously], *The Navy and the Massie-Kahahawai Case,* 37.
30. Pinkerton Detective Agency, Investigation and Report on Ala Moana Case, Summary Volume; also known simply as the Pinkerton Report. It has been available in Lawrence McCully Judd's papers at the HSA for decades. Copies are cataloged at UH's Hamilton Library under the more formal title, "The Ala Moana Assault Case: Investigation Report of the Massie Case."
31. Wright, *Rape in Paradise,* 308.
32. Van Slingerland, *Something Terrible Has Happened,* 318.
33. Wright's and Van Slingerland's works were reviewed by national publications in the 1960s. Lillian De La Torre reviewed both books for the *New York Times Book Review* ("Who Did What to Whom?" September 25, 1966, 3, 42), and *Time* magazine ("The Case That Had Everything," October 7, 1966, 123–124) reviewed *Something Terrible Has Happened.*
34. [Reinecke, anonymously], *The Navy and the Massie-Kahahawai Case,* 1.
35. Wright, *Rape in Paradise,* 304.
36. Ibid., 12.
37. McKillips, "'I've Had to Live with This Thing for 35 Years.'"
38. Okamura, "*Aloha Kanaka, Me Ke Aloha 'Aina,*" 119–137.
39. Ogawa, *Jan Ken Po;* Kotani, *The Japanese in Hawaii.*
40. Ku'umeaaloha Gomes in Mast and Mast, eds., *Autobiography of Protest in Hawai'i,* 426.
41. Ibid., 426–427.
42. Ibid.
43. See the two-part series by Russ and Peg Apple, "'Something Terrible Has Happened,'" *Honolulu Star-Bulletin,* August 4, 1978, A1, and "A Man Is Murdered," *Honolulu Star-Bulletin,* August 11, 1978, A15. See also Lyle Nelson, "Gambling, Narcotics Called HPD's Greatest Challenges," *Honolulu Star-Bulletin,* November 11, 1978, A1; "Massie Case Creates a Stir on the Mainland," *Honolulu Star-Bulletin,* February 17, 1981, A1; and A. A. Smyser, "The Massie Case and Statehood," *Honolulu Star-Bulletin,* March 13, 1984, A16.
44. Letter to the editor by Chris K. Urago, *Honolulu Star-Bulletin,* October 10, 1981.
45. Letter to the editor by John E. Reinecke, *Honolulu Star-Bulletin,* October 14, 1981.
46. Ibid.
47. The *Star-Bulletin* article is "'Something Terrible Has Happened': The Massie Travesty Retold by Lois Taylor," 1981 (n.d. given in book). The editorials come from *Capital Journal* (Salem, Oregon), May 2, 1932; *San Francisco Examiner,* May 2 and 3, 1932; *New York Evening Post,* May 18, 1932; *Chicago Daily News,* May 18, 1932; and *Chicago Tribune,* May 19, 1932.
48. Hurdus, Inn, McKay, and Puzon, developers, *The Shaping of Modern Hawaiian History,* 280.
49. Ibid., 281. *The Shaping of Modern Hawaii* was an extensive undertaking by the Hawaii Multicultural Awareness Project at the University of Hawai'i, College of Education, Curriculum Research and Development Group. Project directors were

Ron Mitchell, 1975–1978, James Harpstrite, 1978–1980, and Eileen Tamura, 1980 to present. Funding was provided by the U.S. Office of Education, Department of Health, Education and Welfare.

50. *The Shaping of Modern Hawaiian History,* 281.
51. Ibid. (italics in original).
52. *Blood and Orchids,* television miniseries.
53. In the introduction to the 1990 Mutual Publishing reprinting of Wright's *Rape in Paradise,* local historian and storyteller Glen Grant comments, "Perhaps the truth would have seemed too fantastic or depressing for a modern audience." Wright, *Rape in Paradise,* v.
54. Wayne Harada, "Familiar Faces in 'Orchids,'" *Honolulu Advertiser,* February 21, 1986, B1–B2.
55. Reyes, *Made in Paradise,* 336–337. The four actors who played the Kauluwela Boys were Robert Andre, Warren Fabro, Russell Omori, and Shaun Shimoda. Lindsey, Haunani Minn, and Henry Kaimu Bal—Hawai'i-born actors working on the continent—also returned to the islands for the filming, bringing to forty-six the total number of actors with connections to Hawai'i.
56. Lindsey produced *Then There Were None,* a video about the declining number of pure-blooded Native Hawaiians; it was nationally broadcast on PBS in 1997 and is discussed in many Hawaiian and Asian American studies courses.
57. Bill Hayden, "Role Touches on Her Own Past," *Honolulu Star-Bulletin,* February 23, 1986, A1, A9.
58. Glen Grant interview, March 21, 1997, Honolulu.
59. Deena Ahakuelo, telephone interview, July 30, 1996, Honolulu.
60. Ibid.
61. Grant interview.
62. I have borrowed this subtitle from a chapter title in Okihiro's book, *Margins and Mainstreams;* Okihiro borrowed it from Paula Gidden's book, *Where and When I Enter: The Impact of Black Women on Race and Sex in America* (New York: William Morrow, 1984).
63. Lipsitz, *Time Passages,* 213.
64. Collins, *Damned in Paradise.*
65. *Honolulu Star-Bulletin,* February 20, 1986.
66. Elizabeth Porteus, "Porteus did not hate members of minorities," *Honolulu Star-Bulletin,* January 16, 1998. Porteus' letter was in response to a viewpoint column by American studies professor David Stannard (*Honolulu Star-Bulletin,* December 12, 1997) that suggested changing the name of Porteus Hall. Several people had been urging the name change since the early 1970s; it was renamed Saunders Hall in 2001.
67. "Testimony of Beverly Ann Deepe Keever," March 4, 1998.
68. David Stannard, "The Massie Case: Injustice and Courage," *Honolulu Advertiser,* October 14, 2001.
69. They included Geoff White, David Hanlon, Vilsoni Hereniko, Haunani-Kay Trask,

Gary Pak, and Rodney Morales, as well as guest speakers like Vince Diaz, Kehaulani Kauanui, and Teresia Teawa.

70. Mark Zwonitzer, personal communication, October 18, 2003, Hartford, Connecticut. I met with Zwonitzer for brunch at an academic panel on the history and literature of Hawai'i. Among other things, I did my best to impress upon him how personal and family connections over the generations make Hawai'i a deeply interconnected place.

71. Cobey Black, telephone interview, July 7, 2010. The three books published in 1966 were Packer and Thomas' *The Massie Case;* Van Slingerland's *Something Terrible Has Happened;* and Wright's *Rape in Paradise.*

72. John Berger, "Trial by Theater: A play on the Massie case will finally see light after being shelved for more than 30 years." *Honolulu Star-Bulletin,* January 8, 2004.

73. Dennis Carroll, personal communication, May 14, 2011.

74. Berger, "Trial by Theater."

75. Play attendance on Sunday, January 11, 2004.

76. For more on the "local" character of *Massie/Kahahawai* and other Kumu Kahua Theatre plays, see Choy, "Staging Identity."

77. Stannard, *Honor Killing* (paperback ed.), 426.

78. Tara Kahahawai, personal communication, August 10, 2006; Aonani Ahakuelo-Chernisky, personal communication, August 11, 2007; May 10, 2012.

79. One of Landgraf's photos appears in Stannard's *Honor Killing.*

80. Guest lectures every September from 2008 to 2011 for SOCS 496, often coordinated by Professor Karen Jolly of the Department of History. Other faculty for the team-taught class during those years included political scientist Kathy Ferguson, anthropologist Alice Dewey, and geographers Jon Goss and Matt McGranaghan.

81. The Department of Education's 2013 high-school graduation requirements include four credits (full years) of social studies that include courses called Modern History of Hawaii (half credit) and Participation in a Democracy (half credit).

82. The University of Minnesota Libraries Clarence Darrow Digital Collection.

83. National Endowment for the Humanities Landmarks of American History and Culture Workshop for Schoolteachers, "Pearl Harbor: History, Memory, Memorial." AsiaPacificEd Program, East-West Center; National Park Service and Arizona Memorial Museum Association, 2007–2009.

EPILOGUE

1. For a discussion of some of the ethnic tensions among locals, see Fujikane's "Between Nationalisms," 23–57.

2. Hine, for example, believes that we cannot fully grasp just how a slave nanny felt, knowing that she was nursing and raising her future oppressors. Hine, "Female Slave Resistance," 123. Another social historian, Deborah White, believes that the dearth of narratives, diaries, and letters makes it almost impossible to draw conclusions about a slave woman's feelings.

3. Gordon, *Ghostly Matters*, 19.
4. "Hawai'i '78 Introduction." Composed by Mickey Ioane. Sound recording from *Facing Future*. Big Boy Record Company, 1993.
5. Sumida, *And the View from the Shore*, 240.
6. Ibid., 240. "Waste time" is a Hawai'i Creole English expression derived from the Hawaiian verb *poho*, to waste.
7. Ibid.
8. Takaki, *Pau Hana*, ix. *Pau hana* is a popular Hawai'i Creole English expression used since plantation days meaning "work is finished."
9. Ibid., 24. Takaki cites Murayama, a novelist, on five separate occasions in *Pau Hana*: 92, 98, 151, 152, and 174.
10. Ibid., 118–119.
11. Chock et al., eds., *Talk Story*.

CHRONOLOGY

1. *New York Herald-Tribune*, July 3, 1963; Van Slingerland, *Something Terrible Has Happened*, 305. Theon Wright dates Massie's death a year earlier, on July 2, 1962. Wright, *Rape in Paradise*, 304.

BIBLIOGRAPHY

UNPUBLISHED MATERIALS

Commandant's Office, 14th Naval District Headquarters, Pearl Harbor. Board of
      Investigation files. Record Group 181, National Archives and Records
      Administration (NARA), San Bruno, California.
———. Clippings file. Record Group 181, NARA, San Bruno, California.
———. General Correspondence, 1925–1942. Record Group 181, NARA, San Bruno,
      California.
Walter F. Dillingham. *A Memorandum,* "For Private Circulation and Not for Publi-
      cation," May 17, 1932. Hawaiian Collection, Hamilton Library, University
      of Hawai'i, Honolulu.
Victor Houston Papers. Hawai'i State Archives (HSA), Honolulu, Hawai'i.
Lawrence McCully Judd Papers. HSA, Honolulu, Hawai'i.
John Kelley Papers. HSA, Honolulu, Hawai'i.
League of Women Voters of Hawaii Papers. HSA, Honolulu, Hawai'i.
Pinkerton Detective Agency. Investigation and Report on Ala Moana Case, Sum-
      mary Volume. [Often referred to as the Pinkerton Report or sometimes as
      "The Ala Moana Assault Case: Investigation Report of the Massie Case."]
      Honolulu, Los Angeles, New York, 1932. HSA, Honolulu, Hawai'i.

PUBLISHED MATERIALS

Adams, Romanzo. Annual Report of the [Honolulu] Police Department. City and
    County of Honolulu, Territory of Hawaii, 1933.
——. "The Education and the Economic Outlook for the Boys of Hawaii: A Study in
    the Field of Race Relationships." Preliminary paper presented at the Second
    General Session of the Institute of Pacific Relations, Honolulu, May 1927.
——. Interracial Marriage in Hawaii: A Study of the Mutually Conditioned Processes
    of Acculturation and Amalgamation. New York: Macmillan Company, 1937.
——. "The Unorthodox Race Doctrine of Hawai'i." In Race and Culture Contacts,
    ed. E. B. Reuter, 143–160. New York: McGraw-Hill and Company, 1934.
Adams, Walter J. "Hawaiian Horror: Behind the Scenes in the Fortescue-Massie
    Case." True Detective Mysteries 18 (1932): 6–13, 80–85.
Akana, Akaiko. Light Upon the Mist: A Reflection of Wisdom for the Future Genera-
    tions of Native Hawaiians. Honolulu: Mahina Productions, 1998.
Amato, Joseph A. Rethinking Home: A Case for Writing Local History. Berkeley:
    University of California Press, 2002.
Anderson, Benedict. Imagined Communities: Reflections on the Origin and Spread of
    Nationalism. Rev. ed. New York: Verso, 1991.
Anthony, J. Garner. Hawaii under Army Rule. Stanford, Calif.: Stanford University
    Press, 1955.
Bacchilega, Cristina. Legendary Hawai'i and the Politics of Place: Tradition, Transla-
    tion, and Tourism. Philadelphia: University of Pennsylvania Press, 2007.
Baker, Ray Stannard. "Human Nature in Hawaii: How the Few Want the Many
    to Work for Them Perpetually and at Low Wages." American Magazine
    (January 1912): 331–333.
Bakhtin, Mikhail. The Dialogic Imagination. Austin: University of Texas Press, 1981.
Beaglehole, Ernest. Some Modern Hawaiians. Honolulu: University of Hawai'i Re-
    search Publications, 1937.
Bederman, Gail. Manliness & Civilization: A Cultural History of Gender and Race in
    the United States, 1880–1917. Chicago: University of Chicago Press, 1995.
Beechert, Edward D. Working in Hawaii: A Labor History. Honolulu: University of
    Hawai'i Press, 1985.
Bell, Roger. A Last among Equals: Hawaiian Statehood and American Politics.
    Honolulu: University of Hawai'i Press, 1984.
Black, Cobey. Hawaii Scandal. Waipahu, Hawai'i: Island Heritage, 2002.
Blanding, Don. Hula Moons. New York: Dodd, Mead & Company, 1930.
Blood and Orchids. Television miniseries. Directed by Jerry Thorpe. Teleplay by
    Norman Katov. Produced by Andrew Adelson. Lorimar Productions,
    1986. Aired on CBS, February 23–24, 1986, in two 2-hour segments.

Bodnar, John. *Remaking America: Public Memory, Commemoration, and Patriotism in the Twentieth Century.* Princeton, N.J.: Princeton University Press, 1992.

Brennert, Alan. *Honolulu: A Novel.* New York: St. Martin's Press, 2009.

Brownmiller, Susan. *Against Our Will: Men, Women and Rape.* New York: Fawcett Columbine, 1975.

Buck, Elizabeth. *Paradise Remade: The Politics of Culture and History in Hawai'i.* Philadelphia: Temple University Press, 1993.

Burrows, Edwin G. *Hawaiian Americans: An Account of the Mingling of Japanese, Chinese, Polynesian, and American Cultures.* New Haven, Conn.: Yale University Press, 1947.

Carroll, Dennis. *Massie/Kahahawai.* Dramatic stage production. Honolulu, 2004.

Chang, Jeff. "Lessons of Tolerance: Americanism and the Filipino Affirmative Action Movement in Hawai'i." *Social Process in Hawai'i* 37 (1996): 115.

———. "Local Knowledge(s): Notes on Race Relations, Panethnicity and History in Hawai'i." *Amerasia* 22 (1996): 1–29.

Chapin, Helen Geracimos. *Shaping History: The Role of Newspapers in Hawai'i.* Honolulu: University of Hawai'i Press, 1996.

Chaplin, George. *Presstime in Paradise: The Life and Times of the Honolulu Advertiser, 1856–1995.* Honolulu: University of Hawai'i Press, 1998.

Charlot, John. *Hawaiian Poetry of Religion and Politics: Some Religio-Political Concepts in Postcontact Literature.* Honolulu: Institute for Polynesian Studies, Brigham Young University-Hawai'i, 1985.

Chock, Eric, Darrell H. Y. Lum, Gail Miyasaki, Dave Robb, Frank Stewart, and Kathy Uchida, eds. *Talk Story: An Anthology of Hawaii's Local Writers.* Honolulu: Petronium Press/Talk Story, Inc., 1978.

Choy, Sammie L. "Staging Identity: The Intracultural Theater of Hawai'i." Ph.D. dissertation, University of Hawai'i, 2011.

Collins, Max Allan. *Damned in Paradise.* New York: Dutton, 1996.

Confino, Alon. "Collective Memory and Cultural History: Problems of Method." *American Historical Review* 102 (1997): 1386–1403.

Coulter, John W., and Alfred G. Serrao. "Manoa Valley, Honolulu: A Study in Economic and Social Geography." *Bulletin of the Geographical Society of Philadelphia* 30 (1932): 109.

Crane, Susan. "Writing the Individual Back into Collective Memory." *American Historical Review* 102 (1997): 1372–1385.

Cuklanz, Lisa M. *Rape on Trial: How the Mass Media Construct Legal Reform and Social Change.* Philadelphia: University of Pennsylvania Press, 1996.

Darrow, Clarence. "The Massie Trial." *Scribner's* 9 (1932): 213–218.

———. *The Story of My Life.* New York: C. Scribner's Sons, 1932.

Daws, Gavan. *Shoal of Time: A History of the Hawaiian Islands.* New York: The Macmillan Company, 1968.

Day, A. Grove. *Books about Hawaii: Fifty Basic Authors.* Honolulu: University Press of Hawai'i, 1977.

de Certeau, Michel. *The Practice of Everyday Life.* Berkeley: University of California Press, 1984.

Dening, Greg. *Mr. Bligh's Bad Language: Passion, Power and Theatre on the* Bounty. New York: Cambridge University Press, 1992.

Du Puy, William Atherton. *Hawaii and Its Race Problem.* Washington, D.C.: U.S. Government Printing Office, 1932.

Elbert, Samuel H., and Noelani Mahoe, eds. *Na Mele O Hawai'i Nei: 101 Hawaiian Songs.* Honolulu: University of Hawai'i Press, 1970.

Enloe, Cynthia. *Bananas, Beaches & Bases: Making Feminist Sense of International Politics.* Berkeley: University of California Press, 1990.

Espiritu, Yen Le. *Asian American Women and Men: Labor, Laws, and Love.* Thousand Oaks, Calif.: SAGE Publications, 1997.

Ethnic Studies Oral History Project (ESOHP), University of Hawai'i. *Kalihi, Place of Transition.* Honolulu: Ethnic Studies Oral History Project, University of Hawai'i, 1984.

——. *Remembering Kakaako: 1910–1950.* Honolulu: Ethnic Studies Oral History Project, University of Hawai'i, 1978.

——. *Waikiki, 1900–1985: Oral Histories.* Honolulu: Ethnic Studies Oral History Project, University of Hawai'i, 1988.

Farrell, John A. *Clarence Darrow: Attorney for the Damned.* New York: Random House, 2011.

Feeser, Andrea, and Gaye Chan. *Waikīkī: A History of Forgetting and Remembering.* Honolulu: University of Hawai'i Press, 2006.

Forgacs, David, ed. *An Antonio Gramsci Reader: Selected Writings, 1916–1935.* New York: Schocken Books, 1988.

Fortescue, Grace. "The Honolulu Martyrdom: Mrs. Granville Fortescue Tells Her Story at Last." *Liberty* (July 30, 1932): 5–10.

Foucault, Michel. *Power/Knowledge: Selected Interviews & Other Writings, 1972–1977.* New York: Pantheon Books, 1980.

Frankenberg, Ruth. *White Women, Race Matters: The Social Construction of Whiteness.* Minneapolis: University of Minnesota Press, 1993.

Franklin, Wayne, and Michael Steiner. "Taking Place: Toward the Regrounding of American Studies." In *Mapping American Culture,* ed. Wayne Franklin and Michael Steiner, 3–23. Iowa City: University of Iowa Press, 1992.

Fuchs, Lawrence. *Hawaii Pono, "Hawaii the Excellent": An Ethnic and Political History.* Honolulu: The Bess Press, 1961.

Fujikane, Candace. "Between Nationalisms: Hawai'i's Local Nation and Its Troubled Racial Paradise." *Critical Mass: A Journal of Asian American Cultural Criticism* 1 (1994): 23–57.

Geschwender, James, Rita Carroll-Seguin, and Howard Brill. "The Portuguese and Haoles of Hawaii: Implications for the Origin of Ethnicity." *American Sociological Review* 53 (1988): 515–527.

Goodman, James. *Stories of Scottsboro.* New York: Pantheon Books, 1994.

Gordon, Avery F. *Ghostly Matters: Haunting and the Sociological Imagination.* Minneapolis: University of Minnesota Press, 1997.

Gramsci, Antonio. *Selections from the Prison Notebooks.* New York: International Publishers, 1971.

Grant, Glen. "Introduction." In *Rape in Paradise* [1966], by Theon Wright. Honolulu: Mutual Publishing, 1990.

Gray, Francine du Plessix. *Hawaii: The Sugar-Coated Fortress.* New York: Random House, 1972.

Griffin, Farah Jasmine. *If You Can't Be Free, Be a Mystery: In Search of Billie Holiday.* New York: One World / Ballantine Books, 2000.

Gulick, Sidney L. *Mixing the Races in Hawaii: A Study of the Coming Neo-Hawaiian American Race.* Honolulu: Hawaiian Board Book Rooms, 1937.

Hall, Stuart. "Cultural Identity and Diaspora." In *Identity: Community, Culture, Difference,* ed. Jonathan Rutherford. London: Lawrence and Wishart, 1990.

Hariman, Robert, ed. *Popular Trials: Rhetoric, Mass Media, and the Law.* Tuscaloosa: University of Alabama Press, 1990.

Hawaii's Last Queen. Television broadcast. Written and produced by Vivian Ducat. WGBH Boston American Experience series, 1997.

"Hawai'i '78 Introduction." Sung by Israel Kamakawiwo'ole. Composed by Mickey Ioane. Sound recording from *Facing Future.* Big Boy Record Company, 1993.

Hawkins, Richard A. "Princess Abigail Kawananakoa: The Forgotten Territorial Native Hawaiian Leader." *Hawaiian Journal of History* 37 (2003): 163–177.

Hine, Darlene. "Female Slave Resistance: The Economics of Sex." *The Western Journal of Black Studies* 3 (1979): 123.

Holmes, T. Michael. *The Specter of Communism in Hawaii.* Honolulu: University of Hawai'i Press, 1994.

Holt, John Dominis. *On Being Hawaiian.* Honolulu: Topgallant Publishing, 1964.

———. *Recollections: Memoir of John Dominis Holt, 1919–1935.* Honolulu: Ku Pa'a Publishing Incorporated, 1993.

Hooper, Paul F. *Elusive Destiny: The Internationalist Movement in Modern Hawaii.* Honolulu: University of Hawai'i Press, 1980.

Hormann, Bernhard L. "The Caucasian Minority." *Social Process in Hawai'i* 14 (1950): 49.

Huang, Yunte. *Charlie Chan: The Untold Story of the Honorable Detective and His Rendezvous with American History.* New York: W. W. Norton & Company, 2010.

Hurdus, Luzviminda, Kristina Inn, Susan McKay, and Julie Puzon, developers. *The Shaping of Modern Hawaiian History: Teacher's Manual.* Edited by Jan Friedson. Honolulu: Hawaii Multicultural Awareness Project for the Department of Education, State of Hawai'i, 1980.

Ige, Philip Keimin. "Paradise and Melting Pot in the Fiction and Non-Fiction of Hawaii: A Study of Cross-Cultural Record." Ph.D. dissertation, Columbia University, 1968.

Ito, Karen L. *Lady Friends: Hawaiian Ways and the Ties that Define.* Ithaca, N.Y.: Cornell University Press, 1999.

James, Bill. *Popular Crime: Reflections on the Celebration of Violence.* New York: Scribner, 2011.

Jardine, John. *Detective Jardine: Crimes in Honolulu.* Edited by Bob Krauss. Honolulu: University of Hawai'i Press, 1984.

Johnson, Donald D. *The City and County of Honolulu: A Governmental Chronicle.* Honolulu: University of Hawai'i Press and the City and County of Honolulu, 1991.

Judd, Lawrence McCully. *Lawrence M. Judd and Hawaii.* Rutland, Vt.: Charles Tuttle Press, 1971.

Kame'eleihiwa, Lilikala. *Native Land and Foreign Desires: Pehea La E Pono Ai.* Honolulu: Bishop Museum Press, 1992.

Kanahele, George Hu'eu Sanford. *Ku Kanaka, Stand Tall: A Search For Hawaiian Values.* Honolulu: University of Hawai'i Press, 1986.

Katov, Norman. *Blood and Orchids.* New York: St. Martin's/Marek, 1983.

Kauanui, J. Kehaulani. "Off-island Hawaiians 'Making' Ourselves at 'Home': A (Gendered) Contradiction in Terms?" *Women's Studies International Forum* 21, November–December (1998): 681–693.

Kawaharada, Dennis. *Local Geography: Essays on Multicultural Hawai'i.* Honolulu: Kalamakū Press, 2004.

Kent, Noel J. *Hawaii: Islands under the Influence.* New York: Monthly Review Press, 1983.

Kneubuhl, Victoria Nalani. *Murder Casts a Shadow: A Hawai'i Mystery.* Honolulu: University of Hawai'i Press, 2008.

Kodama-Nishimoto, Michi, Warren S. Nishimoto, and Cynthia A. Oshiro, eds. *Hanahana: An Oral History Anthology of Hawaii's Working People.* Honolulu: Ethnic Studies Oral History Project, University of Hawai'i, 1984.

Kotani, Roland. *The Japanese in Hawaii: A Century of Struggle.* Honolulu: The Hawaii Hochi, Ltd., 1985.

Landsberg, Alison. *Prosthetic Memory: The Transformation of American Remembrance in the Age of Mass Culture.* New York: Columbia University Press, 2004.

Larson, Edward J., and Jack Marshall, eds. *The Essential Words and Writings of Clarence Darrow.* New York: Modern Library, 2007.

Lili'uokalani, Queen Lydia. *Hawaii's Story By Hawaii's Queen* [1898]. Tokyo: Charles E. Tuttle Company, Inc., 1964.

Lind, Andrew W. *Hawaii's People.* Honolulu: University of Hawai'i Press, 1955.

———. *An Island Community: Ecological Succession in Hawaii.* Chicago: University of Chicago Press, 1938.

———. "Some Ecological Patterns of Community Disorganization in Honolulu." *American Journal of Sociology* 36 (1931): 206–212.

Linnekin, Jocelyn, and Lin Poyer, eds. *Cultural Identity and Ethnicity in the Pacific.* Honolulu: University of Hawai'i Press, 1990.

Lipsitz, George. *The Possessive Investment in Whiteness: How White People Profit from Identity Politics.* Philadelphia: Temple University Press, 1998.

———. *Time Passages: Collective Memory and American Popular Culture.* Minneapolis: University of Minnesota Press, 1990.

Liu, John M. "Cultivating Cane: Asian Labor and the Hawaiian Sugar Plantation System within the Capitalist World Economy, 1835–1920." Ph.D. dissertation, University of California, Los Angeles, 1985.

Lum, Darrell H. Y. "Local Genealogy: What School You Went?" In *Growing Up Local: An Anthology of Poetry and Prose from Hawai'i,* ed. Eric Chock, James R. Harstad, Darrell H. Y. Lum, and Bill Teter. Honolulu: Bamboo Ridge Press, 1998.

MacCannell, Dean. *The Tourist: A New Theory of the Leisure Class.* New York: Schocken Books, 1976.

Malo, David. *Hawaiian Antiquities: Mo'olelo Hawai'i* [1898]. Trans. Nathaniel B. Emerson. Honolulu: Bishop Museum Press, 1951.

Mānoa Valley Residents. *Mānoa: The Story of a Valley.* Honolulu: Mutual Publishing, 1994.

Marchetti, Gina. *Romance and the "Yellow Peril": Race, Sex, and Discursive Strategies in Hollywood Fiction.* Berkeley: University of California Press, 1993.

Marumoto, Masaji. "The Ala Moana Case and the Massie-Fortescue Case Revisited." *University of Hawai'i Law Review* 5 (1983): 271–287.

Mast, Robert H., and Anne B. Mast, eds. *Autobiography of Protest in Hawai'i.* Honolulu: University of Hawai'i Press, 1996.

Matsuda, Mari J., ed. *Called From Within: Early Women Lawyers of Hawai'i.* Honolulu: University of Hawai'i Press, 1992.

Maza, Sarah. "Stories in History: Cultural Narratives in Recent Works in European History." *American Historical Review* 101 (1996): 1493–1515.

Mazón, Mauricio. *The Zoot-Suit Riots: The Psychology of Symbolic Annihilation.*
    Austin: University of Texas Press, 1984.
McGregor, Davianna Pōmaikaʻi. "Kupaʻa I Ka ʻaina: Persistence on the Land." Ph.D.
    dissertation, University of Hawaiʻi, 1989.
———. *Nā KuaʻĀina: Living Hawaiian Culture.* Honolulu: University of Hawaiʻi Press,
    2007.
Melendy, H. Brett. *Walter Francis Dillingham, 1875–1963: Hawaiian Entrepreneur
    and Statesman.* Lewiston, N.Y.: Edwin Mellen Press, 1996.
Morimoto, Lauren Shizuyo. "The Barefoot Leagues: An Oral (Hi)story of Football in
    the Plantation Towns of Kauaʻi." Ph.D. dissertation, Ohio State University,
    2005.
Murayama, Milton. *All I Asking For Is My Body* [1975]. Honolulu: University of
    Hawaiʻi Press, 1988.
Native Hawaiian Resource Center. *Oral Histories of the Native Hawaiian Elderly: On
    the Island of Oʻahu.* Honolulu: Alu Like, Inc., 1989.
Native Hawaiians Study Commission: Report on the Culture, Needs and Concerns
    of Native Hawaiians, Pursuant to Public Law 96-565, Title III. Final
    Report. Volume I, 1983.
Nelligan, Peter J. "Social Change and Rape Law in Hawaii." Ph.D. dissertation,
    University of Hawaiʻi, 1983.
Obeyesekere, Gananath. *The Apotheosis of Captain Cook: European Mythmaking in
    the Pacific.* Princeton, N.J.: Princeton University Press, 1992.
Office of Hawaiian Affairs. *ʻOnipaʻa, Five Days in the History of the Hawaiian Nation:
    Centennial Observance of the Overthrow of the Hawaiian Monarchy.* Hono-
    lulu: Office of Hawaiian Affairs, 1994.
Ogawa, Dennis M. *Jan Ken Po: The World of Hawaii's Japanese Americans.* Honolulu:
    Japanese American Resource Center (JARC), 1973.
Okamura, Jonathan Y. "*Aloha Kanaka Me Ke Aloha ʻAina:* Local Culture and Society
    in Hawaiʻi." *Amerasia* 7 (1980): 119–137.
———. *Ethnicity and Inequality in Hawaiʻi.* Philadelphia: Temple University Press, 2008.
———. "Why There Are No Asian Americans in Hawaiʻi: The Continuing Signifi-
    cance of Local Identity." *Social Process in Hawaiʻi* 35 (1994): 161–178.
Okihiro, Gary Y. *Cane Fires: The Anti-Japanese Movement in Hawaii, 1865–1945.*
    Philadelphia: Temple University Press, 1991.
———. *Margins and Mainstreams: Asians in American History and Culture.* Seattle:
    University of Washington Press, 1994.
———. "Oral History and the Writing of Ethnic History: A Reconnaissance into
    Method and Theory." *Oral History Review* 9 (1981): 27–46.
Omi, Michael, and Howard Winant. *Racial Formation in the United States: From the
    1960s to the 1990s.* 2nd ed. New York: Routledge, 1994.

Owen, Russell. "Hot and Cold." In *We Saw It Happen: The News behind the News That's Fit to Print,* ed. Hanson W. Baldwin and Shepard Stone, 219–220. New York: Simon and Schuster, 1938.

Packer, Robert, and Bob Thomas. *The Massie Case.* New York: Bantam Books, 1966.

Palmer, Albert W. *The Human Side of Hawaii: Race Problems in the Mid-Pacific.* Boston: The Pilgrim Press, 1924.

Panek, Mark. *Big Happiness: The Life and Death of a Modern Hawaiian Warrior.* Honolulu: University of Hawai'i Press, 2011.

Paredes, Américo. *Folklore and Culture on the Texas-Mexican Border.* Austin: Center for Mexican American Studies, University of Texas, 1993.

———. *"With His Pistol in His Hand": A Border Ballad and Its Hero.* Austin: University of Texas Press, 1958.

Park, Robert E. "Race Relations and Certain Frontiers." In *Race and Culture Contacts,* ed. E. B. Reuter. New York: McGraw-Hill and Company, 1934.

———. "Urbanization as Measured by Newspaper Circulation." *American Journal of Sociology* 35 (1929): 60–79.

Peukert, Detlev J. K. "The History of Everyday Life–A Different Perspective." In *Inside Nazi Germany: Conformity, Opposition, and Racism in Everyday Life,* by Detlev Peukert, 21–25. New Haven, Conn.: Yale University Press, 1987.

Picture Bride. Directed by Kayo Hatta. Written by Kayo Hatta and Mari Hatta. Produced by Diane Mei Lin Mark, Lisa Onodera, and Cellin Gluck. Thousand Cranes Filmworks, 1995.

Portelli, Alessandro. *The Death of Luigi Trastulli and Other Stories: Form and Meaning in Oral History.* Albany: State University of New York Press, 1991.

Pratt, Helen Gay. *Hawaii: Off-Shore Territory.* New York: Charles Scribner's Sons, 1944.

Preza, Donovan C. "The Empirical Writes Back: Re-examining Hawaiian Dispossession Resulting from the Māhele of 1848," Master's thesis, University of Hawai'i, 2010.

Puette, William J. *The Hilo Massacre: Hawaii's Bloody Monday, August 1st, 1938.* Honolulu: University of Hawai'i, College of Continuing Education and Community Service, Center for Labor Education and Research, 1988.

Pukui, Mary Kawena, and Samuel H. Elbert, eds. *Hawaiian Dictionary: Hawaiian-English, English-Hawaiian.* Rev. and enl. ed. Honolulu: University of Hawai'i Press, 1986.

Pukui, Mary Kawena, Samuel H. Elbert, and Esther T. Mookini, eds. *Place Names of Hawaii.* Rev. and exp. ed. Honolulu: University of Hawai'i Press, 1974.

Rapson, Richard L. *Fairly Lucky You Live Hawaii! Cultural Pluralism in the Fiftieth State.* Lanham, Md.: University Press of America, Inc., 1980.

Rayson, Ann. *Modern Hawaiian History, Revised Edition.* Honolulu: Bess Press, 1994.

Reinecke, John E. *Language and Dialect in Hawaii: A Sociolinguistic History to 1935.* Honolulu: University of Hawai'i Press, 1969.

———. *A Man Must Stand Up: The Autobiography of a Gentle Activist.* Edited by Alice M. Beechert and Edward C. Beechert. Honolulu: Biographical Research Center, University of Hawai'i, 1993.

——— [anonymously]. *The Navy and the Massie-Kahahawai Case.* Honolulu: *Honolulu Record,* 1951.

Reyes, Luis I. *Made in Paradise: Hollywood's Films of Hawai'i and the South Seas.* Honolulu: Mutual Publishing, 1995.

Robertson, Ben, Jr. "'The Hawaiian Melting Pot.'" *Current History* 36 (1932): 312–315.

Robinson, Lilian S. "The False Claim of Rape and the Liberal Consensus: Sex, Race, and Gender in the Massie and Scottsboro Cases." Paper presented at the 112th Annual Meeting of the American Historical Association, Seattle, Washington, January 10, 1998.

Roediger, David. *The Wages of Whiteness: Race and the Making of the American Working Class.* New York: Verso, 1991.

Rohrer, Judy. *Haoles in Hawai'i.* Honolulu: University of Hawai'i Press, 2010.

Rosa, John P. "Local Story: The Massie Case Narrative and the Cultural Production of Local Identity in Hawai'i." *Amerasian Journal* 26:2 (2000): 93–115.

Rosengarten, Theodore. *All God's Dangers: The Life of Nate Shaw.* New York: Random House, 1974.

Rosenzweig, Roy, and David Thelen. *The Presence of the Past: Popular Uses of History in American Life.* New York: Columbia University Press, 1998.

Ruby, Laura, ed. *Mō'ili'ili: The Life of a Community.* Honolulu: Mō'ili'ili Community Center, 2005.

Sahlins, Marshall. *Islands of History.* Chicago: University of Chicago Press, 1985.

Sai, David Keanu. *UA MAU KE EA: Sovereignty Endures: An Overview of the Political and Legal History of the Hawaiian Islands.* Honolulu: Pū'ā Foundation, 2011.

Sakoda, Kent, and Jeff Siegel. *Pidgin Grammar: An Introduction to the Creole English of Hawai'i.* Honolulu: Bess Press, 2003.

Sánchez, George J. *Becoming Mexican American: Ethnicity, Culture, and Identity in Chicano Los Angeles, 1900–1945.* New York: Oxford University Press, 1993.

Sánchez, Rosaura. *Telling Identities: The Californio Testimonios.* Minneapolis: University of Minnesota Press, 1995.

Schepple, K. L. "Telling Stories." *Michigan Law Review* 87 (1989): 2073–2097.

Schmitt, Robert C. "Survey Research in Hawai'i before 1950." *Hawaiian Journal of History* 21 (1987): 110.

Schudson, Michael. *Watergate in American Memory: How We Remember, Forget, and Reconstruct the Past.* New York: Basic Books, 1992.

Scott, James C. *Domination and the Arts of Resistance: Hidden Transcripts.* New Haven, Conn.: Yale University Press, 1990.

Scott, Joan W. "Experience." In *Feminists Theorize the Political,* ed. Judith Butler and Joan W. Scott, 22–40. New York: Routledge, 1992.

Scott, Shaunna L. *Two Sides to Everything: The Cultural Construction of Class Consciousness in Harlan County, Kentucky.* Albany: State University of New York Press, 1995.

Searles, Patricia, and Ronald J. Berger, eds. *Rape & Society: Readings on the Problem of Sexual Assault.* Boulder, Colo.: Westview Press, 1995.

Silva, Noenoe. "*Kūʻē!* Hawaiian Women's Resistance to Annexation." *Social Process in Hawaiʻi* 38 (1997): 2–15.

Smart, Carol. *Feminism and the Power of Law.* New York: Routledge, 1989.

Stannard, David E. *Before the Horror: The Population of Hawaiʻi on the Eve of Western Contact.* Honolulu: Social Science Research Institute and University of Hawaiʻi Press, 1989.

——. *Honor Killing: How the Infamous "Massie Affair" Transformed Hawaiʻi.* New York: Penguin Group, 2005.

Stillman, Amy K. "Re-membering the History of Hawaiian Hula." In *Cultural Memory: Reconfiguring History and Identity in the Postcolonial Pacific,* ed. Jeannette Marie Mageo, 187–204. Honolulu: University of Hawaiʻi Press, 2001.

Stirling, Yates, Jr. *Sea Duty: The Memoirs of a Fighting Admiral.* New York: G. P. Putnam's Sons, 1939.

Sumida, Stephen H. *And the View from the Shore: Literary Traditions of Hawaiʻi.* Seattle: University of Washington Press, 1991.

Takaki, Ronald. *Pau Hana: Plantation Life and Labor in Hawaii, 1835–1920.* Honolulu: University of Hawaiʻi Press, 1983.

——. *Strangers from a Different Shore: A History of Asian Americans.* New York: Little, Brown and Company, 1989.

Takayama, Eric. "Error in 'Paradise': Race, Sex and the Massie-Kahahawai Affair of 1930s Hawaii." Master's thesis, University of Hawaiʻi, 1997.

Tamura, Eileen H. *Americanization, Acculturation, and Ethnic Identity: The Nisei Generation in Hawaii.* Urbana: University of Illinois Press, 1994.

Tengan, Ty P. Kāwika. *Native Men Remade: Gender and Nation in Contemporary Hawaiʻi.* Durham, N.C.: Duke University Press, 2008.

Territory of Hawaii. *Laws of the Territory of Hawaii Passed by the Sixteenth Legislature, First Special Session, 1932.* Honolulu: Honolulu Star-Bulletin, Ltd., 1932.

——. *Revised Laws of Hawaii, 1925.* Honolulu: Honolulu Star-Bulletin, Ltd., 1932.

"Testimony of Beverly Ann Deepe Keever, Member of the President's Commission on Diversity, Presented to the President's Ad Hoc Committee on Porteus

Hall." March 4, 1998. Available at http://www.hawaii.edu/diversity/keever
.html#note2.

Thompson, E. P. *The Making of the English Working Class*. London: Victor Gollancz,
1963.

Trask, Haunani-Kay. "The Birth of the Modern Hawaiian Movement: Kalama Valley,
Oʻahu." *Hawaiian Journal of History* 21 (1987): 126–153.

———. *From A Native Daughter: Colonialism and Sovereignty in Hawaiʻi*. Monroe,
Me.: Common Courage Press, 1993.

Trujillo, Nick. *In Search of Nanny's Grave: Age, Class, Gender, and Ethnicity in an
American Family*. Walnut Creek, Calif.: Alta Mira Press, 2004.

Tuan, Yi-Fu. "Place and Culture: Analeptic for Individuality and the World's Indif-
ference." In *Mapping American Culture,* ed. Wayne Franklin and Michael
Steiner, 27–49. Iowa City: University of Iowa Press, 1992.

U.S. Bureau of the Census. *Fifteenth Census of the United States: 1930, Outlying
Territories and Possessions, Number and Distribution of Inhabitants, Composition and Characteristics of the Population, Occupations, Unemployment
and Agriculture*. Washington, D.C.: U.S. Government Printing Office,
1932.

U.S. Congress, Senate. *Administration in Hawaii: Hearing before the Committee on
Territories and Insular Affairs*. 72nd Congress, 2nd Session. Washington,
D.C.: U.S. Government Printing Office, January 16, 1933.

———. *Charges Against Official Acts of Judge A. M. Cristy, of Hawaii: Letter from Rudolph Bukeley to Senator Kenneth McKellar, of Tennessee,* 72nd Congress,
1st Session, Document No. 77. Washington, D.C.: U.S. Government Printing Office, April 4, 1932.

———. *Report on Law Enforcement in the Territory of Hawaii,* by Assistant Attorney
General Seth W. Richardson. Washington, D.C.: U.S. Government Printing
Office, 1932. [Known as the "Richardson Report."]

U.S. Department of Justice. *Investigation Concerning Law Enforcement and Crime
Conditions in the Territory of Hawaii*. Unpublished typescript (carbon),
1932. [Fifteen volumes of interviews conducted by Richardson Report
team. Microfilm reels at Hamilton Library, University of Hawaiʻi.]

Valdez, Luis. *Zoot Suit and Other Plays*. Houston: Arte Publico Press, 1992.

Van Slingerland, Peter. *Something Terrible Has Happened*. New York: Harper & Row,
1966.

Vitousek, Roy A. "Functions and Problems of Government in Hawaii." In *University of Hawaii Occasional Papers, paper no. 22*. Honolulu: University of
Hawaiʻi, January 22, 1935.

Walkowitz, Judith R. *City of Dreadful Delight: Narratives of Sexual Danger in
Late-Victorian London*. Chicago: University of Chicago Press, 1992.

——. *Prostitution and Victorian Society: Women, Class, and the State.* New York: Cambridge University Press, 1980.

Weinman, Samuel. *Hawaii.* New York: International Pamphlets, No. 37, 1934.

White, Hayden. *The Content of the Form: Narrative Discourse and Historical Representation.* Baltimore: Johns Hopkins University Press, 1987.

Whitehead, John. "Hawai'i: The First and Last Far West?" *Western Historical Quarterly* 23 (1992): 156.

Whittaker, Elvi. *The Mainland Haole: The White Experience in Hawaii.* New York: Columbia University Press, 1986.

Wiegman, Robyn. *American Anatomies: Theorizing Race and Gender.* Durham, N.C.: Duke University Press, 1995.

Wilkinson, Joseph F. "Look at Me." *Smithsonian* (December 1997): 136–38, 143–151.

Williams, Raymond. *Marxism and Literature.* Oxford: Oxford University Press, 1977.

Wilson, Rob, and Arif Dirlik, eds. *Asia/Pacific as Space of Cultural Production.* Durham, N.C.: Duke University Press, 1995.

Wineburg, Samuel S. *Historical Thinking and Other Unnatural Acts: Charting the Future of Teaching the Past.* Philadelphia: Temple University Press, 2001.

Wooden, Wayne S. *Return to Paradise: Continuity and Change in Hawaii.* Lanham, Md.: University Press of America, 1995.

——. *What Price Paradise? Changing Social Patterns in Hawaii.* Lanham, Md.: University Press of America, 1981.

Wright, Theon. *The Disenchanted Isles: The Story of the Second Revolution in Hawaii.* New York: Dial Press, 1972.

——. *Rape in Paradise.* New York: Hawthorn Books, 1966.

Wyatt, David. *Five Fires: Race, Catastrophe, and the Shaping of California.* New York: Addison-Wesley Publishing Company, Inc., 1997.

Yamamoto, Eric. "From 'Japanee' to Local: Community Change and the Redefinition of Sansei Identity in Hawaii." Master's thesis, University of Hawai'i, 1974.

Yu, Henry. *Thinking Orientals: Migration, Contact, and Exoticism in Modern America.* New York: Oxford University Press, 2001.

Zwonitzer, Mark. *The Massie Affair.* WGBH Boston American Experience series, 2005.

INTERVIEWS AND PERSONAL COMMUNICATIONS CONDUCTED BY THE AUTHOR
(ALL IN HONOLULU UNLESS OTHERWISE NOTED)

Ahakuelo, Deena, telephone interview, July 30, 1996.
Ahakuelo-Chernisky, Aonani, personal communication, August 11, 2007 and May 10, 2012.
Black, Cobey, telephone interview, July 10, 2010.
Blaisdell, Kekuni, personal communication, August 13, 2012.
Carroll, Dennis, personal communication, January 8, 2004 and May 16, 2011.
Christensen, Carl, personal communication, February 11, 2011.
Gomes, Kuʻumeaaloha, interview, August 17, 2010.
Grant, Glen, interview, March 21, 1997.
Hawaii Judiciary Center, personal communication, March 29, 2011.
Hench, Virginia, personal communication, August 2, 2010.
Kahahawai, Tara, personal communication, August 10, 2006.
Kahahawai Farrant, Kim, personal communication, October 21, 2009.
Kaniaupio, Dawn, personal communication, August 1, 2011.
Kurashige, Nicole, personal communication, December 10, 2012.
Leonardi, Luwella, personal communication, October 21, 2009.
Leota, Nicholas, personal communication, October 4, 2010.
Makanani, Kawika, personal communication, January 29, 2011.
McElrath, Ah Quon, interviews, June 28, 1996 and March 14, 1997.
Minatodani, Dore, personal communication, September 5, 2012.
Rodrigues, Darlene, personal communication, May 10, 2012.
Stannard, David E., personal communication, August 17, 2006, April 12, 2010, and April 20, 2012.
Tamura, Eileen, personal communication, March 15, 2011.
Wong, Joseph, personal communication, July 10, 1996, Kula, Maui, Hawaiʻi.
Woolsey Reed, Miriam, interview, March 10, 1997.
Yamauchi, Lois, interview, July 14, 2011.
Yano, Christine, personal communication, October 21, 2009.
Zwonitzer, Mark, personal communication, October 18, 2003, Hartford, Connecticut.

PERIODICALS

American
American Weekly
Capital Journal (Salem, Oregon)
Chicago Daily News
Chicago Defender

Chicago Tribune
Christian Century
Crime and Punishment
Current History
Hawaii Educational Review
Hawaii Herald
Hawaii Hochi (sections both in English and Japanese)
Hilo Tribune Herald
Honolulu Advertiser
Honolulu Record
Honolulu Star-Bulletin
Honolulu Times
Jitsugyo-no-Hawaii (sections in English and Japanese)
Ke Alakai o Hawaii (sections in English and Hawaiian)
Los Angeles Times
Liberty
Maui News
Nation
New York Amsterdam News
New York Evening Post
New York Herald-Tribune
New York Times
Nippu Jiji (sections in English and Japanese)
Paradise of the Pacific
Recorder (San Francisco, California)
San Francisco Chronicle
San Francisco Examiner
Scribner's
Seattle Post-Intelligencer
Survey Graphic
Thrum's Annual (Honolulu, Hawai'i)
Time True Detective
True Detective Mysteries

INDEX

An n after a page number indicates a note on that page.

AAU (Amateur Athletic Union), 16
academia, 78, 97, 104, 108
Adams, Romanzo, 11–12, 58, 59, 128n42
African Americans: and myth of male
    rapist, 120n4; and Scottsboro
    case, 1, 28
Ahakuelo, Benedict "Benny": accusa-
    tions against, 1; actions/move-
    ments on Sept. 12, 22–24; area
    of residence, 19; defense lawyer
    for, 40; friendships with Japanese
    Americans, 59; and Kauluwela
    Gang, 13–14; media portrayals
    of, 16; newspaper interview in
    later life, 85–86; physical prowess
    of, 16; picked up by police, Sept.
    13, 24; on reason police picked
    up Kauluwela Boys, 25; schools
    attended, 19; and sports, 16, 20;
    views body of Joseph Kahahawai,
    49. *See also* Ala Moana assault trial
Ahakuelo, Deena, 93

Ahuna, Robert, 52–53
ahupuaʻa (geographic districts), 18
Akina, Ernest A. K., 49
Ala Moana assault trial: circumstances
    leading to assault, 1, 38–40; de-
    fense lawyers, 40–41; jury mem-
    bers, 40; mistrial, 1–2, 42; mixed
    jury, whites objection to, 61; pros-
    ecution lawyers, 40; responses
    to, 41–43; testimony of Thalia
    Massie, 41; trial, 40–41
Ala Moana Boys, 10, 25
Ala Wai Inn, 17, 38–39
alienists (expert witnesses), 2, 69
aliʻi (chiefly class), 46, 47
All God's Dangers (Rosengarten), 108
All I Asking For Is My Body
    (Murayama), 106
Aloha Amusement Park, 17, 22, 23
"Aloha ʻOe", 53, 54, 127n27
Amateur Athletic Union (AAU), 16
American English, 13

Americanization, 60
American Weekly, 56
Anderson, Benedict, 29
annexation of Hawai'i, 46–47, 55, 57
Ariyoshi, Koji, 83
audiences: academic, 97; continental,
5, 6, 7, 66, 76, 79, 89; general,
82, 91; local, 5, 6, 7, 66, 76, 79,
102; public/community, 66, 78;
university students, 89–91

Bamboo Ridge poets, 115
barefoot football, 16, 20
baseball, 15
Becket, Jan, 98
Bellinger, Eustace (Mr. and Mrs.), 40
Berger, John, 96–97
Big Five firms, 31, 48, 56–57, 63, 65, 67
Bingham, Hiram, III, 82
Black, Cobey, 6, 10–11, 84, 96, 114
Blaisdell, Kekuni, 54–55, 97
Blaisdell, William, 97
Blood and Orchids (novel; Katov), 85,
88, 96, 113, 127n29
Blood and Orchids (television
miniseries), 8, 79, 88, 91–92, 107,
113; rebroadcast of, 94, 114
Bodnar, John, 78
Botello, John G., 40
boxing, 15, 16, 20, 23
Branson, Jerry, 39
Brede, William, 40
Brennert, Alan, 114
Britten, Frederick, 56–57
Brownmiller, Susan, 27–28, 120n4,
130n22
Bukeley, Rudolph, 67
"bull" (leader), 20, 119n37
Burns, James, 93
Burrows, Edwin G., 82–83

Carroll, Dennis, 6, 96–97, 114
Chamber of Commerce, 31, 81, 83

Chang, Henry: accusations against, 1;
actions/movements on Sept. 12,
23; area of residence, 19; defense
lawyer for, 40; and Kauluwela
Gang, 13–14; picked up by police,
Sept. 13, 24; schools attended, 19;
and sports, 20; views body of Joseph Kahahawai, 49. *See also* Ala
Moana assault trial
*Charlie Chan: The Untold Story of the
Honorable Detective and His Ren-
dezvous with American History*
(Huang), 114
Charlot, John, 53
Chinese Americans: electorate, 47, 57;
in Republican Party, 58
Citizens' Organization for Good Government, 36, 42
*Clarence Darrow: Attorney for the
Damned* (Farrow), 115
class. *See* haole elites; Native Hawaiian
elites; working class
collective memory, 8, 78
Collins, Max Allan, 94, 114
commission form of government,
56–57, 83
Communist Party, 83
Correa, Sylvester P., 13, 22, 119n44
Correa luau, 22–23, 24
Coulter, John Wesley, 34, 122n25
countermemory, 94
Cristy, Albert M., 66, 67
cultural geography, of urban Honolulu:
identity and, 17–18, 34–35; zones of
compatibility and competition, 21
cultural nationalism of King Kalākaua,
53–54
cultural productions: documentary,
6, 95–96, 97–98, 100, 114; film,
106–107; historical reenactments,
92–93; *mele* (song), 53–54; novels,
85, 88, 96, 114; play, 6, 96–97, 114;
poetry, 115; television miniseries,

8, 79, 88, 91–92, 94, 107, 113, 114; textbook, 89–91; true-crime books, 11, 84–85, 94. *See also individual works by title*

culture: American, role in development of local culture, 15; military personnel cultural frames of reference, 37–38; Native Hawaiian cultural activities, 54, 56, 103; youth culture, 11–12

curriculum: kindergarten-grade 12 (K-12), 6, 86; university/college, 6, 89–91

Damned in Paradise (Collins), 94, 114

dances, 15, 16, 25; at Aloha Amusement Park, 17, 22, 23

Darrow, Clarence: agrees to become defense attorney, 2, 67; assistants to, 68; closing remarks, 72; criticism by Theon Wright, 84; fee charged by, 67; friendship with Wrights, 84; inability to appear in court, 71–72; misjudgment of racial issues, 73–75; publications by, 81; relationship with media, 69, 131n31; strategy used by, 69, 70–71

Davis, Charles, 2, 69, 72, 73

Davis, Isaac, 55

Davis, Sybil, 23

de Certeau, Michel, 119n39

delinquency/disorganization, spatial patterns in Honolulu, 17–18

Democratic Party, 57, 58, 112

Department of the Interior, 16, 19, 86

Dillingham, Louise, 36, 84

Dillingham, Walter F., 36, 81–82, 83, 84, 89, 128n38

Du Bois, W. E. B., 33

electoral politics, 45, 54, 56

electoral power, of Native Hawaiians, 47–48

elites. *See* haole elites; Native Hawaiian elites

expert witnesses (alienists), 2, 69

Farrow, John, 115

female jurors, push for, 42

Filipino migration, during 1920s and 1930s, 11

Filipinos: class/ethnicity as plantation workers, 106–107; labor strikes by, 12, 117n8

football, 15, 23, 49; barefoot, 16, 20

Fortescue, Grace: area of residence, 19; commutation of sentence of, 2, 61, 74; on life in Hawai'i, 34–35, 37; on nonwhite crime against whites, 35; publications, 80, 81; regret about death of Joseph Kahahawai, 80; role in kidnapping and murder of Joseph Kahahawai, 2, 42–43; sentencing of, 2, 73. *See also* Massie-Fortescue murder trial

Fortescue, Hélène, 37

Fountain, Ernest H., 40

Freitas, Joseph, 39, 123n39

French, Robert, 40

Fuchs, Lawrence, 32

Fukunaga, Myles, 83

Fukunaga case, 18, 83, 87

Gajelonia, Gizelle, 115

gender: and formation of local identity, 27; and patriarchy, 28–29, 130n22; unbalanced sex ratio, 11, 12; and white womanhood, 31, 33, 38–41

Gomes, Ku'umeaaloha, 87–88, 89

Goodman, James, 108

Gordon, Avery, 104–105

Grant, Glen, 77, 79, 92–93

Great Depression, 11, 12, 21, 33, 35, 47

Great Mahele, 46

haole, origin/use of term, 31–32,
    121n17, 121n18
haole elites: and commission form of
    government, 56–57; *kama'āina,*
    6–7, 32, 60, 62; political alliance
    with Native Hawaiians elites,
    57–58, 60–62; relationship with
    Native Hawaiian elites, 47–48. *See
    also* haole population
haole population: distribution of,
    122n24; diversity among, 32; on
    extralegal measures as defense of
    white womanhood, 43; geograph-
    ic segregation of, 29, 34–35; and
    ideology of white domination,
    32–33; *malihini* haoles, 32, 60, 62,
    66; and racial hierarchy, 28; rec-
    reation among, 37–38; structure
    of, 36–37; view on racial tension,
    35–36; and white privilege, 31. *See
    also* haole elites
Hatta, Kayo, 106–107
"haunting," 104
Hawaii, Off-Shore Territory (H. Pratt),
    82
Hawaiian, use of term, 125n2. *See also*
    Native Hawaiians
Hawaiian Americans (Burrows), 82–83
"Hawaiian Horror" (Macfadden), 80
Hawaiian-language immersion schools,
    102
Hawaiian Renaissance, 86–87, 102, 108
Hawaiian Sugar Planters' Association
    (HSPA), 81–82, 106
Hawai'i Creole English (HCE), 118n13;
    colonial dialect, 13–14; creole
    dialect, 13. *See also* pidgin
Hawaii Hochi, 56, 57, 62–63, 74, 83,
    84, 87
"Hawai'i Pono'ī" (anthem), 53–54,
    127n24
Hawaii's Scandal (Black), 6, 114
Heen, William, 40

Hee Wai, 40
Hine, Darlene Clark, 104, 135n2
historical narrative: and closure, 75–76;
    plot, as source of embarrassment,
    76
historical reenactment of Massie case,
    92–93
history: *mo'olelo,* 46, 54; oral history,
    77–78, 103, 108, 132n6; public
    history, 6, 8, 77–78, 99. *See also*
    memory
Hiura, Arnold, 93
Holt, John Dominis, 108
Home Rule Party, 60
Honolulu (Brennert), 114
Honolulu Advertiser, 30, 35, 36, 37, 43,
    48, 49, 63, 87, 91, 95
Honolulu Chamber of Commerce, 31,
    81, 83
Honolulu Magazine, 98
"Honolulu Martyrdom" (Fortescue), 80,
    132n9
Honolulu Record, 67, 83–84
Honolulu Star-Bulletin, 30, 48, 49–50,
    61, 63, 83, 85–86, 87, 89, 90, 91,
    94
Honolulu Times, 35, 37
Honor Killing (Stannard), 6–7, 98, 100,
    114
Houston, Victor, 42, 82
Howes, Craig, 97
Huang, Yunte, 114

Ida, Horace: accusations against, 1;
    actions/movements on Sept.
    12, 22–24; area of residence, 19;
    defense lawyer for, 41; and Kau-
    luwela Gang, 13–14; kidnapping
    and beating of, 2, 42, 50; picked
    up by police, Sept. 13, 24; rebel-
    lion by, 15; schools attended, 19;
    and sports, 20; traffic accident
    with Peeples, 24–25; views body

of Joseph Kahahawai, 49. *See also*
Ala Moana assault trial
identity. *See* local identity
immigration restrictions, 57
Indian captivity narratives, 27–28
intermarriage, 59, 128n42
International Longshoremen's and
Warehousemen's Union (ILWU),
83
Iwilei, ethnic make up of, 21, 22

James, Bill, 115
Jamieson, Gill, 83
*Jan Ken Po: The World of Hawaii's Japa-
nese Americans* (Ogawa), 87
Japanese/Japanese Americans: citi-
zenship after annexation, 47;
class/ethnicity as plantation
workers, 106–107; electorate,
57, 58; friendship with Native
Hawaiians, 58–59; and intermarriage, 128n42; labor strikes by,
12, 117n8; in Mānoa, 34; racism
against, 62–63, 73–74, 83, 87;
reaction to beating of Horace
Ida, 50; women, as live-in maids,
122n25. See also *Hawaii Hochi*;
Ida, Horace; *Jitsugyo-no-Hawaii*;
Nippu Jiji; Takai, David
*The Japanese in Hawaii: A Century of
Struggle* (Kotani), 87
Jitsugyo-no-Hawaii, 30
Jones, Albert Deacon: commutation of
sentence of, 2, 61, 74; confesses
to killing Joseph Kahahawai, 85;
hired by Massie family to protect
Thalia, 33; role in kidnapping and
murder of Joseph Kahahawai, 2,
42–43; sentencing of, 2, 73. *See
also* Massie-Fortescue murder
trial
Judd, Lawrence McCully: commutation
of sentences in Massie-Fortesuce

case, 2, 7, 61, 74; and law enforcement reform, 36, 42, 49,
83; and mainland coverage of
Massie-Fortescue case, 81–82;
moves up sentencing date in
Massie-Fortesuce case, 73; and
Pinkerton Report, 80–81; publishes memoirs, 86; regrets commuting sentences, 79–80; updating
of files on Massie-Fortescue case,
81–82
justice and racial divide, 61–62, 83
juvenile delinquency, 18, 19

Kahahawai, Joseph "Kalani": accusations against, 1; actions/move-
ments on Sept. 12, 23–24; area
of residence, 19; attends private
school, 19, 52; defense lawyer
for, 41; friendships with Japanese
Americans, 59; funeral of, 44,
48–49, 52–54; funeral of, fear of
riot, 49–51; and Kauluwela Gang,
13–14; kidnapping and murder of,
2, 42–43, 124n59; kidnapping and
murder of, response to, 51–52;
media portrayals of, 16; physical
prowess of, 16; picked up by police, Sept. 13, 24; and sports, 16,
20. *See also* Ala Moana assault
trial
Kahahawai, Joseph, Sr., 51–52
Kahanamoku, Duke, 71
Kai, Ernest, 41
Kaikapu, Lui, 30, 43, 121n11
Kaka'ako: ethnic make up of, 21, 22;
social disorganization in, 18
Kaka'ako Gang, 19
Kalākaua (King), 53, 127n32
Kalaniana'ole, Jonah Kūhiō, 60, 63
Kalihi, social disorganization in, 18
Kalihi Gang, 15, 19
Kalihi-Pālama (Kapālama), 98; ethnic

makeup of, 21–22; social class in, 18–19

Kalili, Maioli, 62

Kalili, Manuela, 62

Kama, David, 44, 48, 61–62

kama'āina, 6–7, 32, 60, 62

Kamakau, Samuel, 46

Kamakawiwo'ole, Israel, 104, 105

Kamehameha the Great, 46, 53–54, 55

Kanae, Margaret, 23

Kanahele, George, 108

kanaka maoli piha (pure-blooded Native Hawaiians), 59

Kapi'olani Community College, 93

Katov, Norman, 85, 88, 91, 96, 113, 127n29

Kauluwela Boys, 10, 120n56. *See also* Ahakuelo, Benedict "Benny"; Chang, Henry; Ida, Horace; Kahahawai, Joseph "Kalani"; Takai, David

Kauluwela Gang, 13–14, 15, 19

Kawananakoa, Abigail, 47, 55–56, 61, 63, 92, 127n29

Kawananakoa, David, 47, 55, 127n32

Ke Alakai O Hawaii, 49

Keever, Beverly, 95

Keliinoi, Sam, 56

Kelley, John C., 2, 68, 70, 72, 73, 125n61

Kelly, Marion, 100

King, Fay, 37

Kluegel, Anne, 36, 42

Kluegel, Henry, 36

Kotani, Roland, 87

Kuamoto, Takeo, 40

Kumalae, Jonah, 49

labor strikes, 12, 117n8

Landgraf, Kapulani, 98

land tenure reorganization, 46

Lane, John C., 49, 60

law enforcement reform, 36, 41–42, 49, 83, 124n56

League of Women Voters, 36, 41–42, 55, 56, 61

Leavitt, H. H., 51

Lee, Jan Yip, 40

legal system, call for changes in, 42

Leisure, George, 67, 68, 74, 94

Leong, Lavonne, 98

Liberty magazine, 80, 81

Lili'uokalani (Queen), 46, 54, 55, 92, 104, 127n27, 127n32

Lind, Andrew, 5, 17–18, 21, 33, 76

Lindsey, Elizabeth, 91

Lipsitz, George, 78, 94

local identity: construction of, 11–13; and cultural geography of urban Honolulu, 17–18; as cultural identity, 66, 103; emotive elements of, 103–105; and gender, 6, 27; and geographic space and place, 6, 14, 17–18, 21, 29, 34–35; language and construction of, 13–14; and local/mainlander boundary, 66; as oppositional, 12, 28; origins of, 5–7, 76; and political economy, 104; and race, 6, 27, 28, 60; as resistance, 59–60; and social class, 5–6, 60, 76

localism, and social movements of 1970s and 1980s, 86–87

locals: as actors in *Blood and Orchids* miniseries, 91; boundaries with white elites, 66; and recreation, 20–21, 22. *See also* youths

Lord, Edward: commutation of sentence of, 2, 61, 74; hired by Massie family to protect Thalia, 33; role in kidnapping and murder of Joseph Kahahawai, 2, 42–43; sentencing of, 2, 73. *See also* Massie-Fortescue murder trial

Lyman, Daniel, 121n11

lynch law, 51, 80

Macfadden, Bernarr, 80
Mahele, 46
mainlanders: attitudes toward locals, 29;
    boundary with locals, 66
Majors, James, 83
Majors-Palakiko case, 83
maka'āinana (working class Native Ha-
    waiians), 46, 47
malihini haoles, 32, 60, 62, 66
Malo, David, 46, 77, 78
Mānoa Valley, 18–19, 34–35, 99
martial law, 82
Martin, Peter, 20, 21, 119n34
Marumoto, Masaji, 73–74, 76, 87
Massie, Thalia (Bell): agency of, 29–30;
    area of residence, 19; on death of
    Joseph Kahahawai, 43; later life
    and death, 85; provides police
    with license plate number, 25;
    testimony to police, 1, 26, 39–40.
    See also Ala Moana assault trial
Massie, Thomas: area of residence, 19;
    commutation of sentence of, 2,
    61, 74; role in kidnapping and
    murder of Joseph Kahahawai,
    2, 42–43; sentencing of, 2, 73;
    threats to sue over productions of
    Massie case, 96. *See also* Ala Moa-
    na assault trial; Massie-Fortescue
    murder trial
The Massie Affair (PBS documentary;
    Zwonitzer), 6, 95–96, 97–98, 100,
    114
The Massie Case (Packer and Thomas),
    84, 85
Massie-Fortescue murder trial: alle-
    gations of tampering by judge,
    67; and alleged abortion, 70, 71;
    closing arguments, 71; commu-
    tation of sentences, 2, 61, 74; cost
    of defense, 67; expert witnesses
    (alienists) in, 2, 69; grand jury
    indictment, 65, 66; grand jury

returns "no bill," 66; jury selec-
    tion, 68; lack of narrative closure
    for locals, 75–76; as local story,
    4–5; location of trial, 65–66;
    material evidence, 68; and race re-
    lations, 73–75; temporary insanity
    plea, 69; testimony by Thalia
    Massie, 70–71, 72; testimony by
    Thomas Massie, 69–70; trial as
    social event, 69; verdict, 73
Massie/Kahahawai (play; Carroll), 6,
    96–97, 114
Matsugama, Matsuo, 40
Matsumoto, Tatsumi "Tuts," 23
McElrath, Ah Quon, 96, 97
McIntosh, John, 25, 26, 39, 41
McKellar, Kenneth, 67
McKinley High School, 19
media: bias in coverage of rapes, 30–31;
    coverage of Joseph Kahahawai
    funeral, 48–51; coverage of
    Massie-Fortescue murder trial,
    68, 69, 72, 74, 75; editorials
    against white establishment, 65;
    on elite society, 37; on Hawaiian
    royal family, 55–56; Japanese
    American, 30; portrayal of Native
    Hawaiians as savage brutes, 16;
    as promoter of changes in law
    enforcement, 36; racialization
    of working class youth by, 35;
    on racial judicial system, 62–63;
    racism in, 83, 89; on television
    miniseries, 91
mele (song), 53–54
A Memorandum (Dillingham), 82
memory(ies): based on firsthand
    knowledge of Massie case, 78–79,
    80; based on retellings of Massie
    case, 79; collective memory, 8,
    78; countermemory, 94; crucial
    role in examining the past, 78–79;
    failings of, 78; post-World War

II published accounts, 82–84; publications during martial law period, 82; public memory, 78; true-crime books, 78, 84–85; use of technology to store and transmit, 78

military personnel: cultural frames of reference of, 37–38; economic and social effects in Hawai'i, 33; historical basis of animosity of locals toward, 87–88; increase in numbers in Hawai'i, 11, 31, 33; social class position of, 33

Mills, Harry T., 49
missionaries, 15, 31, 32–33, 46, 55, 108
moku (geographic districts), 18
mo'olelo (story, history), 46, 54
Moran, Bill, 83
Murakami, Robert, 40–41
Murayama, Milton, 106
Myles Fukunaga case, 62–63
myth of African American male rapist, 120n4

Napoleon, Walter, 97
The Nation, 51
Native Hawaiian elites, 54, 55; commonalities with working-class, 63–64; political alliance with haole elites, 57–58, 60–62; reaction to murder of Joseph Kahahawai, 59–60; relationship with haole elites, 47–48. *See also* Native Hawaiians
Native Hawaiian Home Rule Party, 57
Native Hawaiians: agency and modes of resistance, 45–48; demographics of, 54–55; diversity among, 54, 55; electoral politics and cultural activities, 54, 56; electoral power of, 47–48, 57; friendship with Japanese Americans, 58–59; number of registered voters, 58; pure-blooded, 59; reaction to

beating of Horace Ida, 50; revival of cultural traditions of, 103; U.S. citizenship for, 47. *See also* Native Hawaiian elites
The Navy and the Massie-Kahahawai Case (Reinecke), 83–84, 89, 100
Navy Night, 38–39
Nelligan, Peter, 36
New York American, 81
New York Mirror, 81
New York Times, 69
Nippu Jiji, 48, 50, 75, 87

O'ahu, concentration of white population on, 31
Odowda, Mrs. James, 30, 42, 43, 121n11
Ogawa, Dennis, 87
Okamura, Jonathan, 5, 12
Okawa, Richard, 106
Okihiro, Gary, 32, 134n62
oral history, 77–78, 103, 108, 132n6
Organic Act in 1900, 47
organized crime, absence of, 19
Oriental vote, 47, 58, 128n40

Packer, Robert, 11, 84, 85
Paikuli, William E., 40
Palakiko, John, 83
Pālama, social disorganization in, 18
Pālama Gang, 15, 19
Paredes, Américo, 121n17
patriarchy, 28–29, 130n22
Pau Hana: Plantation Life and Labor in Hawaii (Takaki), 106, 107
Peeples, Agnes, 24, 25
Peeples, Homer, 24–25
People magazine, 94
Pettengill, George, 50
Picture Bride (film; Hatta), 106–107
pidgin, 13, 14, 118n13
Pinkerton Detective Agency, 80
Pinkerton Report, 80–81, 84, 90, 133n30

Pittman, William, 41, 124n49

place/space: defining, 119n39; and identity, 6, 14, 17–18, 21, 29, 34–35

plantation system: historical fiction on, 106–107; and origins of local identity, 12–13

poems/poetry, about Massie case, 115

Popular Crime (James), 115

Porter, John E., 71

Porteus, Elizabeth, 95

Porteus, Stanley, 95

Portuguese, 34, 39, 68, 119n34, 119n40; as "Caucasian" in U.S. Census, 121n15

Pratt, Helen, 82

Pratt, William, 28, 51

The Presence of the Past, 99

Prohibition, 22, 39, 71

Protect Kaho'olawe 'Ohana group, 87

Puaaloa, John, 23

public history, 6, 8, 77–78, 99

public memory, 78

Puea Cemetery, 98, 126n9

Punahou school, 13

race/ethnicity: justice and racial divide, 61–62, 83; and local identity, 6, 27, 28, 60; and myth of African American male rapist, 120n4; race relations and Ala Moana assault trial, 87–89; race relations and Massie-Fortescue case, 73–75; racialization of crime, 35; racialization of working-class, 35; and rape narrative, 27–30; and segregation, 13, 29, 33, 34–35; white/whiteness (*see* haole population)

racial hierarchy, 27–29, 28, 34, 43

racism: against Japanese, 62–63, 73–74, 83, 87; in media, 83, 89; of U.S. Navy, 63, 89

rape: changes in laws, 42; and myth of

African American male rapist, 120n4; and race of victim, 30. *See also* Ala Moana assault trial

Rape in Paradise (T. Wright), 30–31, 32, 74–75, 84; reprint of, 94, 98

rape narrative: as both local and national story, 28–29; race and agency of victim, 29–30; as rationale for violence, 27–28; as reflection of racial hierarchy, 27–29, 28

recreation: and haole population, 37–38; and locals, 20–21, 22; and plantation workers' children, 12. *See also* dances; sports

Reed, Miriam Woolsey, 77–78, 93

Reinecke, John E., 13, 83–84, 89, 100

renshi (linked poem), 115

Republican Party, 57–58, 60–62, 63

Republican Women's League of Hawaii, 56

Republic of Hawaii, 46

resistance, 62–64

Richardson, Seth W., 80

Richardson Report, 19, 80

Rigby, James "Red," 39

Rohrer, Judy, 32

Roosevelt High School, 13

Rosa, Vasco, 68

Rosengarten, Theodore, 108, 132n6

Rosenswieg, Roy, 99

Ross, Gordon, 74

Rowlandson, Mary, 27

schools/schooling: English Standard schools, 13, 14; ethnicity of faculty in, 14; Hawaiian-language immersion schools, 102; Kauluwela Elementary, 10, 14, 19; non-Standard English school, 14, 19; private schools, 19, 52. *See also* University of Hawai'i

Scottsboro Boys case, 1, 28

Scribner's magazine, 81

Sea Duty (Stirling Jr.), 81
segregation, 13, 29, 33, 34–35
Seki, "Buster," 22
Serrao, Alfred Gomes, 34, 122n25
sex ratio, unbalanced, 11, 12
*The Shaping of Modern Hawaiian
    History* (textbook), 89–91
Shaw, Nate, 132n6
Silva, George, 23
Smart, Carol, 130n22
social activities. *See* dances; recreation
social class. *See* haole elites; Native
    Hawaiian elites; working class
softball, 20
Something Terrible Has Happened (Van
    Slingerland), 31, 84
sports: barefoot football, 16, 20; base-
    ball, 15; boxing, 15; football, 15,
    23, 49; and identity, 20–21; soft-
    ball, 20
Stannard, David E., 10–11, 32, 95–96,
    97–98, 99, 100, 114; on Massie
    affair as prelude to revolution,
    6–7
Star-Bulletin. See Honolulu Star-Bulletin
statehood, 7, 76, 89, 90, 112
stereotypes, 62
Stirling, Yates, Jr., 28, 50–51, 66, 67, 81
St. Louis School, 19, 52
Stogsdall, Ralph, 39
Stone, John, 73
Stories of Scottsboro (Goodman), 108
story/storytelling, and culture of
    history, 3, 4
suffrage, after annexation, 57
Sumida, Stephen, 105
Sylva, Eddie, 40

Takai, David: accusations against, 1;
    actions/movements on Sept.
    12, 22–24; area of residence, 19;
    defense lawyers for, 40–41; and
    Kauluwela Gang, 13–14; picked

up by police, Sept. 13, 24; schools
    attended, 19; and sports, 20; views
    body of Joseph Kahahawai, 49.
    See also Ala Moana assault trial
Takaki, Ronald, 32, 106, 107
talking story, 3, 5, 105–108
Talk Story conference, 105
Taylor, Lois, 89
territoryhood, 47
*The Territory of Hawaii v. Ben Ahakuelo,
    et al. See* Ala Moana assault trial
*Territory of Hawaii v. Massie, Fortescue,
    Lord, and Jones. See* Massie-
    Fortescue murder trial
Thirteen Ways of Looking at the Bus
    (Gajelonia), 115
Thomas, Bob, 11, 84, 85
Thompson, Frank, 68
Three Kings Murder Case. *See*
    Fukunaga case
Thurston, Lorrin P., 81, 83
Trask, Haunani-Kay, 96
true-crime books, 11, 79, 84–85, 94
True Detective Mysteries magazine, 80
Tyssowski (Mrs.), 13–15, 19

Ulrich, Barry, 68
unemployment, 12, 19
University of Hawai'i: courses on
    Massie-Kahahawai case, 100;
    ethnic studies at, 86–87, 96;
    founding of, 34; panels on *Massie/
    Kahahawai* play, 97; renaming of
    Porteus Hall, 95
Urago, Chris, 89

Van Slingerland, Peter, 11, 31, 67,
    84–85, 96
Vierra, Robert, 23–24
Vineyard Street Gang, 15, 19

Walkowitz, Judith, 130n22
Watson, D. W., 9, 10, 59

Watson, John, 40
Weeber, Charles F., 16, 83
Westernization, 55
WGBH Boston: American Experience
    series documentary, 6, 95–96, 97;
    Web page, 100
White, Hayden, 75–76
white hysteria, 30
white/whiteness. *See* haole population
white womanhood, Massie case as
    defense of, 31, 33, 38–41
Wiegman, Robyn, 121n5
Wight, Griffith, 40
Wilbur, Ray Lyman, 16
Wilder, Therese, 83
Wilhelmina Rise case, 30, 43, 121n11
Withington, Paul, 71
women: female jurors, 42, 61; slave
    women, 135n2; use of women's
    bodies before the law, 130n22;
    white womanhood, 31, 33, 38–41;
    women's groups and crime, 36
working class: of color, solidarity of,
    44–45; and English Standard

public schools, 13; and Great
    Depression, 47; Native Hawaiian
    elites' commonalities with, 63–64;
    need for recording stories of, 106;
    neighborhoods in Honolulu, 17,
    21, 29; racialization of, 35; and
    recreation, 20–21, 22
Wortman, Ward, 66, 73, 81
Wright, George Williams, 76, 84
Wright, Theon, 11, 25, 30–31, 32,
    74–75, 84, 85, 94, 120n47

Yamamoto, Eric, 5, 76
Young, John, 55
Young, Kanalu, 96
youths: criminalization of, 20; emer-
    gence of youth culture during
    1920s and 1930s, 11–12; Native
    Hawaiian friendship with Japa-
    nese American, 58–59; relation-
    ship with servicemen, 16–17

Zwonitzer, Mark, 6, 10–11, 95–96, 97,
    98, 99, 114, 135n70

ABOUT THE AUTHOR

JOHN P. ROSA is an assistant professor of history at the University of Hawai'i at Mānoa. After earning his Ph.D. in history at the University of California at Irvine, he taught Asian Pacific American studies at Loyola Marymount University in Los Angeles and at Arizona State University in Tempe. He also taught history at the secondary school level at Kamehameha Schools, Kapāla-ma. His research focuses mostly on the history of modern Hawai'i and the histories of Asian Americans and Pacific Islanders in the United States. He was raised in Kaimukī and Kāne'ohe on the island of O'ahu.